Post-Traumatic God

Post-Traumatic God

How the Church
Cares for People
Who Have Been to
Hell and Back

DAVID W. PETERS

 Morehouse Publishing
NEW YORK

Unless otherwise noted, the Scripture quotations contained herein are from the New Revised Standard Version Bible, copyright © 1989 by the Division of Christian Education of the National Council of Churches of Christ in the U.S.A. Used by permission. All rights reserved.

Morehouse Publishing, 19 East 34th Street, New York, NY 10016

Morehouse Publishing is an imprint of Church Publishing Incorporated.
www.churchpublishing.org

Cover art © 2015 by Melissa McWilliams

Cover design by Jenn Kopec, 2Pug Design

Typeset by PerfecType, Nashville, TN

Library of Congress Cataloging-in-Publication Data
Names: Peters, David W., author.
Title: Post-traumatic God : how the church cares for people who have been to hell and back / David W. Peters.
Description: New York : Morehouse Publishing, 2016. | Includes bibliographical references.
Identifiers: LCCN 2016019853 (print) | LCCN 2016024875 (ebook) | ISBN 9780819233035 (pbk.) | ISBN 9780819233042 (ebook)
Subjects: LCSH: Post-traumatic stress disorder--Patients--Religious life. | Post-traumatic stress disorder--Religious aspects--Christianity.
Classification: LCC BV4910.45 .P48 2016 (print) | LCC BV4910.45 (ebook) | DDC 261.8/324--dc23
LC record available at https://lccn.loc.gov/2016019853

Printed in the United States of America

For my grandfather William C. Prestin (1914–67)
652nd Bomb Squadron, US Army Air Forces, World War II

CONTENTS

PREFACE

After reading so many insightful and compelling books about combat trauma, war, PTSD, and moral injury, you can imagine my hesitancy about adding another one to the already thick canon. Still, I went ahead with the project for a number of reasons. First, many readers of my first book, *Death Letter: God, Sex, and War* told me they wanted to know what happened between the end of the book and the epilogue. They wanted to see how I worked on the theological problems I expressed in the book and how I found healing. Second, as I came home from war I was constantly on the lookout for theology written by people who experienced war. In some way, I suppose, I wrote the book I wanted to read back then. Indeed, many excellent writers on war never "saw the elephant," and many who did see him do not reflect on it theologically in writing. The closest book I found was by German journalist turned theologian, Uwe Siemon-Netto. In 1990 he wrote *The Acquittal of God: A Theology for Vietnam Veterans.* His work as a journalist in Vietnam, Veterans Administration chaplain, and theologian make this book of 100 pages a lifeline for the warriors of his generation. I hope *Post-Traumatic God* can be the same for this generation, the Generation Xers and Millennials who fought these wars in Iraq and Afghanistan. Third, my life is living proof the Church cares for veterans and can heal the wounds of war. I am passionate about equipping churches to do this ministry in their communities. By offering solutions that are theological, penitential, liturgical and sacramental, this book shows that God's people already have what it takes to be part of God's healing mission to veterans.

I am not a psychiatrist or psychologist. Therefore, I do not diagnose anyone with any mental health disorders. In this book I write about post-traumatic stress disorder (PTSD). I realize that many people in the veteran community are dropping the "D," instead focusing on how PTS/PTSD is a normal response to horrific events and images. While I appreciate how dropping the "D" is a step toward destigmatization, I have retained it in this book. The main reason is because the American Psychiatric Association's Diagnostic and Statistical Manual of Mental Disorders (DSM-5) still has it. Nothing more or less is meant by my usage of PTSD.

While I typed each word of this book, many, many others composed the stories and themes in sand, in mud, and in blood. Here are the ones who come immediately to mind:

I am so thankful for Melissa McWilliams who provided the art for the cover. I served with Melissa in Iraq and saw firsthand the hardship of her deployment. She is an example of a warrior who returned to create beautiful things for humanity.

My fellow Marines who learned war with me at Parris Island, South Carolina, and showed me how much physical and psychological strain warriors can endure. Semper Fi. I am also thankful for the women and men of the 62nd Engineer Combat Battalion (Heavy), especially Kurt Stein who shared life with me in Iraq. I was young there, but you were even younger. I am proud to have been your chaplain and hope to be for the rest of our lives.

The wounded warriors and staff at Walter Reed Army Medical Center in Washington, DC, were there for me during my homecoming and I am thankful. I learned so much from you as you recovered physically, emotionally, and spiritually from the blasts of war. Officiating at your weddings and seeing you thrive are some of the happiest moments of my life.

I am thankful for being selected to serve as instructor at the US Army Chaplain Center and School at Ft. Jackson, South Carolina. The army reserve chaplains I teach and mentor remind me the Chaplain Corps is in good hands and the women and men of our armed forces have access to quality spiritual care wherever they may go.

At every meeting or service of the Episcopal Veterans Fellowship the depth of the participants' insights, as well as their sense of humor, amaze me. Each of you has directly influenced how I think about war, homecoming, and community. It has been a blessing to know and journey with each of you. While my personal stories in this book are true, I have intentionally changed the names and identifying details of every other person. Some characters are composite characters of two or more people to protect their privacy.

I have been following Jesus since I was a child and I am glad he led me to be a priest in The Episcopal Church. Serving at the altar is always a vision of heaven for me, and I am grateful to the clergy of The Episcopal Church who made this possible. The Revs. Stuart Kenworthy, Gene Tucker, and David Scheider shepherded me through my ordination process. Thanks for never giving up on my call and always reassuring me it would work out. Thanks to the Rt. Rev. Daniel Martins who agreed to ordain this oft-moving active duty army chaplain. At my ordination, he expressed the beauty of catholic ecclesiology when he said, "This ordination is for the whole church." I am also thankful to the Rt. Rev. James Magness, Bishop Suffragan of the Armed Forces and Federal Chaplaincies. It has been an honor to serve as one of his chaplains in the field as well as hear him preach at both my ordination and marriage to Sarah. Thanks to The Most Rev. Katharine Jefferts Schori and her husband Dr. Richard Schori, who visited me at Walter Reed and affirmed my ministry there. At present, I am thankful for the Rt. Rev. C. Andrew Doyle who empowered me to start the EVF in his diocese as well as the Diocese of Texas' suffragan bishops, The Rt. Revs. Dena Harrison and Jeff Fisher, who continually encourage me to give my best to God's people here in Texas.

I wrote most of this book while serving as the Curate at Grace Episcopal Church in Georgetown, Texas, and later as the Assistant Rector at St. Mark's Episcopal Church in Austin. Both my rectors, the Revs. Trey Garland and Elizabeth Turner, provided cover for me to continue to build up the veteran fellowship and the people of both parishes showed me how liturgy and listening can heal the wounds we all carry.

During the writing of this book, I was enrolled as a student in the Master of Arts in Religion degree program at Seminary of the Southwest, an Episcopal seminary, in Austin. The theological insights of my professors, the seminary's dean, The Very Rev. Cynthia Briggs Kittredge, continually encouraged me to work hard on this project and have faith in God as well as my readers.

I have nothing but thanks for this book's editor, Richard Bass. From our first meeting on the front lawn of the Washington National Cathedral, his insights into the writing process, publishing, and the reading public nurtured this project until its completion.

Lastly, and most importantly, I am grateful for my family. My sister and brothers have always given me a hug when I needed it. My two sons from my first marriage, Soren and Avery, were born shortly after 9/11, and have experienced the challenging lives of being children in an army at war. They are kind, smart, and fun people, and they have taught me so much about grace and love.

I am thankful for my parents, who I know as Dad and Mom. Just a few days after I arrived home from Iraq, I called them in tears and they listened to me. They loved me through the long hours of those dark days and never gave up on me. I have attended dozens of "sending off" ceremonies in the army, and so I have seen many parents send their children off to war. After hearing so many parents confess their worry over their self-destructive veteran daughters and sons, I have seen a glimpse of what parents go through after a deployment to war. They have a burden I have not yet known. I know my parents went through all this, and I hope they know how much I respect and love them.

Today, at the heart of my family is my wife Sarah, an art historian and artist foundation director. She has walked with me through many of my post-traumatic trials, and I know it has not been easy. Just as veteran and priest, the Rev. Christian Hawley, prayed at our wedding, she has been a strength in need, a counselor in perplexity, a comfort in sorrow, and a companion in joy. I have been, at times, very needy, and she has been strong. I have been very perplexed, and she has listened to me and insisted I go to a licensed counselor. I have been sorrowful, and she has comforted me with her words and silence. Together, we have had so much joy, I often think I am living a better life than I could have ever imagined.

The opinions in this book are those of the author and in no way represent the official positions of the US Army Chaplain Corps, the Department of Defense, or the United States government.

David W. Peters
The Feast of Pentecost, 2016

To Hell and Back

I can't ever remember being young in my life.
                                        —Audie Murphy

The subtitle for this book comes from the 1955 film, *To Hell and Back*, starring Audie Murphy, one of the most decorated soldiers of all time. In the film, a very youthful thirty-one-year-old Murphy played himself in a swashbuckling tale of a country boy turned hero in World War II. He earned a million dollars from the film and starred in a number of westerns. After he died in a 1971 plane crash, a different picture emerged of his life.

Medical records from his release from active duty indicated vomiting, nightmares, and other indicators of combat fatigue, now known as post-traumatic stress disorder (PTSD). We now know he self-medicated his symptoms with drugs and alcohol, and reports of violence towards his first wife and more alarming behaviors have surfaced. As a war hero and media celebrity, it was hard for those who idolized him to believe such a great man could have so many demons. Perhaps no one knew. Perhaps no one wanted to know. He had, after all, pitched a sequel to *To Hell and Back* called *The Way Back*, which chronicled his homecoming, but no one wanted to finance it.

The army I served in adored Audie Murphy. Formed at Fort Hood, Texas, a base where I served for four years, the Sergeant Audie Murphy Club is an elite organization devoted to developing competent leaders for the army. To enter the club, a soldier must stand before several examining boards, answering questions to demonstrate proficiency. One of the areas of examination is Murphy's biography. Only the official biography can be used, however. To my knowledge, Murphy's PTSD, his self-medication, or any of his trials of homecoming are completely omitted. The founders of the club felt that good army leaders needed only to know his service number, how many films he starred in (forty-four), and his military awards for bravery. It is little wonder our warriors feel stigma and shame when they struggle in their post-war odyssey.

But Murphy did go to hell and back, and one of his many songs captures the loneliness of his condition.

> Shutters and boards, cover the windows of the house
> Where we used to live
> All I have left, is a heart full of sorrow
> Since she said, she'd never forgive
>
> The house that we built, was once filled with laughter
> But I changed that laughter to tears
> Now, I live in a world without sunshine
> Ooh, I wish you were here
>
> Shutters and boards, cover the windows of the house
> Where we used to live
> All I have left, is a heart full of sorrow
> Since she said, she'd never forgive
>
> Last night I dreamed that you came to our house
> To take an old book from the shelf
> If you'll open the shutters, I'll tear down the boards
> 'Cause I drove every nail by myself

Ever since I came home from the war in Iraq, I see the world differently. At first, I thought the world had changed. Later, I realized I had done the changing. Now, for better or worse, I see everything, including God, through this post-traumatic lens. In this book I will argue I am not alone in this post-traumatic vision of God. Although my trip to hell and back cost me dearly, this post-traumatic vision of God is a good thing, a thing that will bring about more human flourishing. The Church needs this post-traumatic vision of God if she is to bring reconciliation and healing to a wounded world.

Our English word "trauma" is the Greek word for "wound." The purpose of war is to produce trauma in the enemy. Whether the enemy is killed or wounded matters little. All that matters is neutralization of the opposing fighting force. In fact, wounding enemy troops is preferable to killing them since wounded combatants require care by other troops. The dead require very little.

In the United States today, there are several million veterans of the wars in Iraq and Afghanistan. Many of us are wounded physically, psychologically, emotionally, and spiritually. Sometimes, all four of these categories of wounds exist in the same veteran. Each one of us is different and veterans should interpret their own experiences in combat and homecoming. I only know what I went through in Iraq. I only truly know my own experience, and the fog of war shadows that experience. I have forgotten some events for years, only to be reminded of them in a conversation with another veteran. In this book I offer you my experience in war and homecoming, with the hope my story might resonate with veterans and those who love and care for them.

One of the memories that keeps coming back to me happened in a Humvee between Baghdad and a forward operating base (FOB) south of the city. The vehicle had a .50 caliber machine gun mounted on the roof and a soldier in the turret on high alert. The roads were dangerous, and every car, pile of trash, or dead donkey could be concealing an improvised explosive device (IED).

On the way back from the mission, we passed through an Iraqi Army checkpoint on Route Tampa, the main highway from Baghdad to Kuwait. As we approached the checkpoint, a young Iraqi Army soldier, our ally, was having a heated discussion with an old Iraqi man. It looked like they were delaying the passage of the old man's small Toyota truck. The old man was dressed in a long, off-white, traditional Iraqi dress. As we approached the checkpoint, the young soldier stopped talking to the old man. He turned toward us, the approaching American convoy, and looked right at my vehicle. He had a defiant look on his face and I could see his eyes rest on my chaplain assistant as she sat in the passenger seat. She may or may not have noticed his gaze as she scanned the area for IEDs and other threats. Her M16A2 rifle was ready and the .50 Cal on the roof's turret remained silently vigilant. The young soldier looked at her, then he looked at me, and then he punched the old man in the stomach. The robe billowed around the soldier's fist until his fist hit the old man's stomach. The old man crumpled in a heap and we drove on. We always drove on. To stop anywhere was too risky.

There, in what was probably the least violent event of the whole Iraq War, something happened to me. Was this where my God died? I cannot be sure, but I know something shifted inside of me. I think about this moment often as I reflect on my time in Iraq. I think about what I could have done differently. I think of how helpless I was to help the old man. I think about how much effort we were all giving to "fix Iraq." This moment made the whole place seem unfixable.

Worse events surrounded this roadside punch, a few of which I describe in my first book, *Death Letter.* I try not to get too close to these stories anymore since I have found they often obscure what I want to say about war. Many veterans find it hard to talk about war. For me, this comes from my inability to probe the feelings of the event, feelings of failure and regret for not preventing that big bad thing from happening.

The wound in my soul, the moral injury, was in my powerlessness to do good in a bad situation. It was as if I threw the cruel punch, or, at least, approved of that punch, yea, blessed that punch. Moral injuries are the things done and left undone, and these are legion in a war. War is an upside-down moral universe where the good is bad and the bad is good. In this world, the morality we learned as children is suspended. "Don't hit your brother." "Don't hit your sister." Everyday cruelties abound and I was part of them, blessing them.

Now, every time a vehicle I am riding in slows down on the highway, I start to get anxious. The threat of ambush or attack was high in Baghdad and the chances of attack went up when we slowed down because we were lost or in traffic. This feeling is at its worst when the evil hours begin, at twilight. I start a fight with my wife who is driving or complain about little things until the people who are with me begin to feel my anxiety. Never stop, not for anything, is the mantra by body lives by. My inner ear knows to trigger the alarm bells when it feels the slow-down.

I had power in Iraq, more power than I ever had in my whole life. I was part of a team who had the power of life and death. We could kill and get away with it. We could kill and earn awards and medals for it. The only one in the whole universe who has the ultimate power to take a life is God. Except in war. There, in war, an eighteen-year-old woman or man has that power. In the world of war, we were the goddesses and gods.

But that world ended when we came home and the power ended with it. It took a while for me to realize what I lost in Iraq. Sometimes I think it was my innocence. Other times I know it was my god-like power.

When I got home from Iraq, my now ex-wife was having an affair with the neighbor. It took me months to figure that out. I was so out of touch with what was happening around me. I was powerless to save our marriage. In that powerlessness, I came to believe God was powerless too. When I asked, he refused to answer. So much for the deal we had made. So much for the covenant I had kept.

Fear crept into my soul. What I had believed was no longer true. There was no longer any safety with God. There was no longer any safety in the universe. War removed, for me, the illusion that the world is a safe place. I lived with this illusion before combat, but after I saw the elephant, the illusion died with the young men and women who believed it. All illusions die, I suppose. Some die in explosions and other bleed out slowly without even a whimper.

When I arrived in Iraq, we were told to come up with a plan to kill everyone we met. I was a chaplain, usually the only one without a weapon, so I relied on my chaplain assistant. The chaplain assistant was an ordinary soldier assigned to protect the chaplain among other more administrative tasks. Even though she was there with me, I still had to be ready for anything at all times. In a few days, I grew used to this state of affairs. I grew numb to the danger from the people around me and from the roads of Baghdad.

In spite of my comfort with the uncomfortable, the need to escalate my rage was always smoldering under the surface. Soldiers have to go from zero to sixty in a blink of an eye if they hope to survive the unpredictable dangers of war. This stayed with me when I came home. I rarely felt safe and little things would set me off into a paranoid rage. It was as if the lid of civilization had been taken off the boiling cauldron of my own internal struggles. I quickly found that alcohol calmed me down and I began to use it like medicine, in large doses.

The infidelity in my marriage, and the subsequent divorce, flipped everything in my life upside down. I was angry at everything and everyone, including God. I felt that God had betrayed me. I felt that since I had been a faithful husband, a good soldier, a loving chaplain, and a good Christian, God would hook me up with a good marriage. The divorce reinterpreted my whole year in Iraq. My service in Iraq was no longer a noble event in my life. Now, it represented the lull before the storm. With the failure of the marriage, the losses, the deaths, the tears, the dust, and the punches no longer seemed worth it. In this time, I found that traumatic events have the power to change the entire story of our lives. They can make memories of happy times full of ominous foreboding. When my divorce rewrote the story of my Iraq deployment, I realized I had been living under a delusion of happiness the whole time. Now the war represented the breakup of my family and the loss of my primary identity.

The first assignment I was given in the army after Iraq and divorce was a year of clinical pastoral education (CPE) at Ft. Lewis, Washington. There, while my internal identity recalibrated, I found I could no longer write "God" with a capital letter in my papers. All I could do was write "god." This raised some eyebrows in my CPE group, but my colleagues were understanding. Most of them had just returned from Iraq too and were recalibrating their theological framework. In the religious community of my youth and young adulthood, this would have been rank heresy.

This lower-case god did not have the rules of the God I grew up with. This god did not regulate sex like the God of my youth. At the time I did not know I was wounded, and that this is often what a wound looks like. I was on a quest to find a new way to relate to God, with the hope that I could still exist and work as a Christian minister. I liked being with people as they struggled with the trials of life, but I could no longer work for the God I no longer believed in. My search for the post-traumatic God was driven by necessity, not by curiosity. This book contains what I found.

The God Who Disappears

*The courage to be is found in the God who appears when God
disappears in the anxiety of doubt and fear.*

—Paul Tillich

The God of my childhood came to me in stories. Most of these stories
were from the Bible, while others were from the life experiences of
my parents and other people in my church. The stories in the Bible told
me God was powerful and he intervened in his creation quite frequently.
This intervention was backed up by the testimonies of my fellow parishioners. God provided for people in financial hardship, he healed sick
people with doctor-defying suddenness, and he prevented people from
having car crashes and other accidents.

Furthermore, God was always a "he." The maleness of God came
through in almost every story and lesson. God was a king up in heaven.
God ruled over the world and was at the top of every flow chart and chain of
command. His maleness emphasized his strength and power. In Jesus, his
power was limited by the incarnation, only to resurge after the resurrection.

God was a warrior king who destroyed his enemies whether they be
the Canaanites or Egyptians. This same warrior king re-emerged in the
book of Revelation to kill so many of his enemies. The blood flowed up to

the horse's bridle. So much killing and so much death was to be expected if you opposed this God.

We spent a great deal of time explaining the bad things in the world through our theological lenses. Sometimes sickness or tragedy was God's judgment. Sometimes it was God's "chastening." God was punishing us like a loving parent punishes his or her child. God's punishment of us reinforced my community's reliance on corporal punishment, specifically "spanking." Just as God the Father was responsible to discipline his way-ward children, so fathers were to discipline their rebellious children.

During my entire childhood I never heard God speak to me. At least not in the way I heard it described around me. In weekly Wednesday night prayer meetings, the women and men of the church would share testimonies of their conversations with God. God was telling them to talk to that stranger about Jesus, or to be more patient when their water heater broke for the third time.

People died too. They died old and they died young. In these situations we were told that sometimes God allows bad things to happen in this world. Cancer, Parkinson's, or a car wreck could happen because it is a sinful, fallen world. It started with Eve's disobedience in the Garden of Eden and the curse that followed when Adam listened to her. "It's a cursed world" was repeated, mantra-like, in the aftermath of tragedy.

Today, as I look back on the church of my childhood, I am impressed by their tenacity. The faithful wrestled with the biggest theological issue of our modern age daily. They tried to tell a coherent story that took into account every single story in the Bible, the tragic events of our world, and their own dependence on the God they worshiped. This is not easy to do.

Like most Protestants descending from the Reformation, they punted to God's sovereignty. When the tragedy was too personal, they turned to the inscrutable wisdom of God. God had a purpose for every ugly event. What that purpose was remained a mystery.

The dominant story about God was the story of Jesus's crucifixion. This story was told and retold as it shaped my understanding of God. The short version is that God created the world good. Man sinned and God was forced to punish them infinitely, since he is an infinite being. Only Jesus, a perfect man and fully God, could pay the infinite price God demanded. In the courtroom of the universe God is the judge and he demands the death of all sinners. When his son dies on the cross, the sinners' debts are paid.

On this point the Christians I grew up with had no small disagreement. Some said Jesus died for everyone's sins, and all we had to do was accept that fact to receive the benefits of his death. Others said he died only for the elect, the ones chosen by God before creation. If you believed, that proved you were one of these elect. I am obviously oversimplifying a massive corpus of theological distinctions here between Calvinism and Arminianism. As a child, adolescent, and young man I had to make sense of all of this somehow. I was probably better at it then than I am now. In any case, I lived in this tension my whole childhood, never sure which was the better explanation.

The story of the courtroom drama of salvation was preached from the pulpit in the church and on the streets in Philadelphia. We shared it with people door to door every Sunday afternoon, just like the Jehovah's Witnesses. This story embedded this powerful God in my theological imagination. This was the God I took with me to war.

The God I took to war was a God who was pro-civilization. The Protestant reformers were not only concerned with correct theology, they were also concerned with creating an orderly and godly society. Calvin's Geneva shines as one of these examples of this theological-political experimentation. An orderly God is concerned with the orderliness of humanity. I picked up on this early on. God punished or chastened sinners, both Christians and non-Christians, and he wanted us to obey our teachers, parents, and pastors.

God was not only orderly, God was forgiving. He would forgive you if you broke his law, as long as you repented. He could forgive you because Jesus paid your debt on the cross for your sins. Stories of God's forgiveness abounded. At a camp one summer, the week's preacher told us tales of his wild youth. Once, after a night of drinking and driving, he was pulled over by a cop. As the cop approached the car, the drunk young man contemplated killing the police officer with the bat that lay on the floor of the pickup truck. As he thought about killing the cop, he realized he needed to stop living like this. He went back to church, got saved, and started preaching.

The men who told me about this forgiving God were sinners, until they got saved. In my memory they seemed to all be men. They were leaving behind lives of premarital sex, drinking, and violence. They were our heroes. I knew I could never be like them since I grew up in the tame confines of the church. I never drank, never smoked, and never had sex. What could I repent of besides my bad attitude and not tucking in my shirt after gym class?

I realize now my descriptions of my childhood are caricatures of how things really were. This was the only world I knew, so I absorbed all of it unquestioningly. I think children in any number of religious traditions do this. We all move from the concrete to the abstract. Many people move from the certain to the mysterious. In this book I attempt to make the case for how trauma enables us, even forces us, to do just that. For me, it was the trauma of Iraq and homecoming that pushed me into this gray beyond. It is not a tidy or neat process because someone has to die.

God has to die. The God of our childhood has to shatter in a thousand pieces, die, disappear, or change, if we are to have a spiritual life beyond our childhood. This is, of course, from our vantage point. What happens in the heavens or down below is anyone's guess. I just know how I experienced the post-traumatic God.

A Shattered God

Hell rages around us. It's unimaginable.
—Paul Tillich in a letter to his father
during the Battle of Verdun

War has always been a shattering experience. The bombs, rockets, grenades, and bullets used in modern warfare shatter buildings, vehicles, bodies, and even souls. The exposure to and participation in the toxic, traumatic, and deeply disturbing events of war produce psychological wounds, the most common being post-traumatic stress disorder. PTSD is on the rise among veterans returning from Afghanistan and Iraq. The Veterans Administration (VA) estimates that over twenty-one percent of combat veterans suffer from PTSD. Veterans with PTSD consume almost twice as much general health care as those without a clinical mental health diagnosis.

Psychological manuals associate a host of symptoms with PTSD including numbing, detachment, absence of emotional responsiveness, a foreshortened future, a reduction in awareness of surroundings, depersonalization, and dissociative amnesia. One can only imagine how these demons could affect relationships. I experienced numbness in the months of my homecoming from Iraq. Like most numb people, I was unaware of my numbness. The numb world was the normal world I adjusted to in Iraq. There is not an easy way to turn this shift off.

Self-medication with drugs and alcohol (itself a drug) empowers the numbing and sabotages recovery. Before my service in Iraq, I drank very little. During my years in the Marine Corps, I did not drink at all because of my religious convictions. The church of my childhood demanded complete abstinence from alcohol and I conformed. I tried a Coors Light when I was about twenty-four, and had another when I was twenty-six. After I came home from Iraq, my drinking began to accelerate. As I danced between piercing anxiety and comfortable numbing, the alcohol kept the whole program running.

After a night of hard drinking coupled with anxiety, I crashed my bicycle on a curb and broke at least one rib. I woke up in my apartment with little memory of the accident. The drinking had worked for a while, but not forever. While drinking is the most common self-medication for PTSD, grief, and trauma experiences, the dosage increases eventually lead to broken relationships and broken ribs. The day of reckoning had arrived.

Recent scholarship on PTSD abounds. I have learned so much from the scholars and warriors who have engaged this topic. Many have investigated how PTSD, moral injury, and combat trauma affect spirituality. Ed Tick, a psychiatrist working with veterans with PTSD, describes PTSD as an identity wound of the soul that affects the personality at the deepest level. In his book, *War and the Soul,* he shows how wars are fought in the mythic realm of good versus evil. This can leave combatants with complex spiritual wounds. War shatters and reorganizes a person's identity and this is confusing.

During World War I, while serving as a German army chaplain in the bloodiest battles of the war, Paul Tillich repeatedly used the German word, *Erschuetterungen,* "shattered," to describe the war around him in his letters and sermons. Many years after the war he wrote these words: "There are soldiers who have become prophets, and their message is not very different from the message of the ancient Hebrew prophets. It is the message of the shaking of the foundations." Only those who knew what happened to him in World War I knew he was speaking of himself. War shakes the foundations, war shatters relationship, and war creates prophets.

Paul Tillich was a soldier who became a prophet. Like the Hebrew prophets of old, Tillich experiences war and loss, boldly speaking to the issues of his day. He served in the German army during World War I and was exiled by the Nazis shortly before World War II. He was an American citizen during the Korean conflict and the beginning of the Vietnam War. I believe these experiences give him a unique insight into the theological solution to the shattering effects of war that veterans feel. We will return to Tillich's work later, but first, let us examine the shattering effects of war in Scripture.

The Hebrew Bible and the Shattering Effects of War

Your right hand, O LORD, glorious in power—your right hand,
O LORD, shattered the enemy.

—Exodus 15:6

I read the Bible differently now with my post-traumatic vision. I read everything differently now, as do many of the veterans I serve. The veterans in your church may read Scripture differently too. It's worth asking them about this. It's worth listening to them about this.

War was invented by brothers. When Cain killed Abel, war began. Ever since that first fratricide, war has been a human activity. The brother against brother myth has been a dominant theme in the history of warfare. All war is brother against brother because we all share a common humanity, contained in the theological concept of the *imago dei*. God speaks in Genesis 1:26 saying, "Let us make humankind in our image." The concept of the *imago dei* is the beginning of biblical anthropology. Humans have intrinsic worth because we are made in God's image. While *imago dei* can be interpreted in a variety of ways, many theologians agree it contributes to an elevation of human dignity and worth. War is only possible when we refuse to see our fellow humans as image-bearers of the divine. We must dehumanize the enemy so we can kill them.

One of the first books I read about PTSD was by Larry Dewey, a devout Mormon psychiatrist at the VA medical in Boise, Idaho. After years of working with traumatized World War II and Vietnam veterans, he wrote *War and Redemption,* a book that attempts to show how PTSD is primarily a grief issue. He writes that humans go to war first because of propaganda. We go to war because we perceive a threat to ourselves, our way of life, our women, and our culture. Truth and error are mixed together on the images that scare us enough to spring into action. The major theme of the propaganda is always a less than human enemy. The inhumane, un-human enemy will not fight fair, by established rules, or with conventional weapons. They will do hideous things to us, unspeakable things, so we must kill them. The atrocities are always on the other side of the ocean.

Cain killed Abel and was exiled by God to wander the earth. Only those who die in war do not wander after war. The story of Cain and Abel in the first chapters of Genesis demonstrates how war and violence shatter relationships and create disconnection. Cain's mark is one of protection, not stigma, but he is never the same again. Indeed, those who participate in the violence of war are marked by it forever. Like Cain, we "settle in in the land of Nod, east of Eden." But Nod is not a place a man can settle in. It is simply the word for "wanderer" or "exile" in Hebrew. It is a sick joke, a pun on Cain's new title, "Wanderer."

From this first act of violence, humans entered a world where differences are settled by killing. Old Testament scholar Bruce Vawter shows the contrast between the violent humans and the peaceful animals in Genesis by saying, "Mankind is the only species within the order of creation that systematically destroys and preys upon itself out of envy, greed, selfish unconcern, or denial of its own commonality."

The poetry of Scripture captures the feelings of warriors and those who are hurt by war. In David's "Song of the Bow" in 2 Samuel 1, he laments the death of King Saul and Prince Jonathan, his dearest friend, who fell in battle. His strong emotion focuses on the love he felt for Jonathan. Jonathan and David fought together and formed the strongest of bonds that are only forged in combat. While we go to war for propaganda, writes Dewey, we stay in war for love. We endure the trials of combat because of the love we have for each other. I know firsthand the truth of this. I am overcome with emotion when I think of my closest friend from Iraq and what we went through. In the moment we did not know we were forming such a strong connection. It's awkward at times—two men loving each other this much. Bob Dylan, in his haunting song about the Civil War, concludes his final verse, "We loved each other more than we dared to tell." When someone dies in war, or after, the lovers die too. David sings of this in his song and I read it, fully knowing what he is saying.

In the biblical narrative, the military strength established by the wars of David becomes fragile in the civil war and enemy invasions that follow Solomon's reign. The central location of Israel and Judah in the ancient Near East created a situation where they were constantly threatened by their neighbors who grew more powerful every year. Revolts, invasions, and palace intrigue repeated themselves in endless succession in 2 Chronicles 20, 22, and 33. In the midst of this chaos, the prophets emerge as voices of condemnation and hope. Their lives and words called people to social change. In return, the prophets were mocked and persecuted, but never ignored.

As the kingdoms of Israel and Judah were assaulted from all sides, several stories emerged in which Yahweh acted on behalf of his people by single-handedly defeating their enemies. These stories may have reminded the people that Yahweh was still doing the kinds of miracles that are recorded in the earlier days of Israel's history, notably the events of the Exodus.

Few prophets suffered as much grief and loss from war as Jeremiah. His visions of war emphasized the civilian losses from an invasion. "The whole city shall flee from the noise of the horsemen and bowmen. They shall go into thickets and climb up on the rocks. Every city shall be forsaken and not a man shall dwell in it." In this passage in his fourth chapter,

Jeremiah has a vision of God "shaking the foundations" of the earth. It is a destructive power that dismantles the earth in the reverse order of its creation. It was from this passage of war's destruction that Paul Tillich preached his sermon, "The Shaking of the Foundations." This eventually was turned into a book by the same title. Like the prophets of old, Tillich saw possibilities for renewal after the devastations of war. In the sermon he reminds the listener that although scientists promised an age of peace, prosperity, and progress, it was their inventions that brought worldwide destruction. He knew this from his experience in World War I, where advances in machine-gun and poison-gas technologies were felt by the young men on both sides.

In the sermon, he shows how humans practice idolatry by trusting in the visible, tangible foundations of the earth. When war shattered this earthly foundation, this idol, then the real foundation of God's eternal kingdom could be seen. At the end of the sermon he urged his listeners to see, by faith, the solid, eternal rock of salvation, which cannot be destroyed.

Shortly after I arrived at Walter Reed to work as a chaplain on the orthopedic (amputee) and psych wards, I was given a print of Rembrandt van Rijn's *Jeremiah Lamenting Over the Destruction of Jerusalem*. I hung it on my wall because it was a thoughtful present and because I had nothing else to hang on my office wall after my divorce. I had gotten rid of so many things in my self-destructive spiral.

For those three years I looked at it often, as I came and went from visiting the most severely wounded warriors from Iraq and Afghanistan. It became for me an icon of the grieving warrior. Rembrandt portrays Jeremiah seated, with the city of Jerusalem burning in the background. Jeremiah's posture betrays the feelings of defeat and discouragement the losing side feels after a war. His left arm is propped up on a giant Bible. He cannot read it, but only use it as an armrest. I saw this posture often at Walter Reed. I saw it when I looked in the mirror too.

The most significant aspect of the painting for me, however, was Jeremiah's right arm and leg. Although Jeremiah is wearing a rather full robe, he does not have a right arm or right leg. Perhaps this echoes Psalm 137: "If I forget you, O Jerusalem, may my right hand forget her skill" (KJV). Since I was providing pastoral care to numerous amputees, Jeremiah's missing limbs took on a new meaning for me. Everyone loses something in a war, and the arms and legs of the young have become visceral symbols of how combat changes people forever.

The history of Israel is a history of war. Resources were scarce in the ancient world and neighbors often fought over food and water rights. The Minor Prophets reflect the major and minor conflicts of their day with dramatic language. The overwhelming theme of their imagery is destruction. Zephaniah, in the first chapter, focuses on the Day of the Lord as "[a] day of trumpet and alarm against the fortified cities" (NKJV). The Day of the Lord will result in the blood of men "being poured out like dust."

In 1916, German Chief of Staff Erich Von Falkenhayn wrote to the Kaiser and urged him to approve his plan to attack Verdun. He said this action would "Bleed the French white." Thus the brutal war of attrition began that resulted in the deaths of hundreds of thousands of men, women, and children. When he was thirty years old, Chaplain Paul Tillich was at Verdun and wrote to his father saying, "Greetings from the world of iron, fire, and blood." This is the language of war, dramatic, and full of violent imagery and threat. In the Minor Prophets, Yahweh is often the warrior who deals out this kind of judgment.

In modern war, the war I experienced, the explosions from the munitions are beyond enormous. Words alone cannot describe them and they cannot be fully captured on film. Perhaps poetry is the only way to feel what happens when the world becomes a flash of fire. Perhaps the prophets best knew how to tell the story that cannot be told.

The Prophet Zechariah's message about the Day of the Lord has Yahweh promising to "[g]ather all the nations to battle against Jerusalem; the city shall be taken, the houses rifled and the women raped." Yahweh becomes both the agent of violence and the agent of restoration. Yahweh is first the divine warrior who is celebrated throughout the Hebrew Bible in poems and songs. Yahweh promises to restore the land so that "[t]he people shall dwell [in Jerusalem] and no longer shall there be utter destruction, for Jerusalem shall be safely inhabited." The ancient prophets were very aware of war's destructive power, as well as the dramatic restoration and re-creation that can follow that destruction.

It is good to know I am not alone in feeling the poetry of war in the texts of Scripture. They speak to me in a language I can understand all too well. They show the moral upside-down universe of war and the moral injury, discouragement, and depression that follows the sounds of the guns. The God that these documents witness to understands the warring part of human life better than we know, at least, better than contemporary Christianity is often willing to admit.

The New Testament and the Shattering Effects of War

Then Pilate wondered if he were already dead; and summoning the centurion, he asked him whether he had been dead for some time.

—St. Mark 15:44

The New Testament was written during the *Pax Romana,* a period of relative peace and security in the ancient Near East. The symbols of Roman occupation in Palestine were everywhere, and the Jews who authored the New Testament were very conscious of this reality. The only military operation in the four gospels was the crucifixion of Jesus. These documents witness the shattering effects of occupation, a subject I can relate to intimately.

I was part of an occupying army in Iraq. Armies occupy to benefit the people they are occupying, at least that is what the armies always say. We occupied Iraq to bring them democracy, security, and freedom, all lofty ideals. In reality, our occupation created innumerable situations where humans suffered. Our military dominance over the people of Iraq was very visible and physical. We did this for our own safety, because we were scared of being killed, but it normally served only to separate us further from the people we were there to help and partner with.

If we drove through Baghdad during the day, we would put sirens and police lights on our Humvees so the traffic would clear out of our way. If they didn't clear, or if the cars were so backed up in front of us, we would drive over the median curb and drive in the oncoming lane. No one dared get in our way because we were allowed to shoot any vehicle that felt like a threat with a .50 caliber machine gun. It worked. It kept us relatively safe, but all one would have to do was look at the blank faces of the Iraqi drivers to know we were not winning hearts and minds. The stories of families shot up because they were driving too close to our convoys are numerous and follow us back to the states. The ghosts of Iraq are often in vehicles.

The Centurion in St. Mark's gospel would likely have much in common with the sergeant major I served with in Iraq. In spite of this, Mark puts the confession that Jesus is the Son of God in the mouth of the Centurion who is in charge of the crucifixion. In contrast to the fickle, uncertain governor Pilate, the soldiers in the Gospels are decisive and honest, if not terribly cruel.

Like the prophets of the Hebrew Bible, Jesus predicted the destruction of Jerusalem by a military force in Matthew 24 and Luke 21. Jesus said the "[h]eavens will be shaken" and the Temple will be destroyed, and "[n]ot one stone left upon another." He goes on to preach, "Nation will rise against nation" and the violence will destroy the earth. Then Jerusalem will be surrounded by armies and be trampled underfoot. The holy city will be shattered. Again, Jesus echoes a familiar theme of war shattering places and lives; however, when it is all over, "Raise your heads, because your redemption is drawing near." War shatters, but from that shattering comes re-creation and redemption.

The climax of apocalyptic war imagery is found in the *Revelation of Jesus Christ According to John*. The destruction and devastation poured out on the earth reaches epic proportions. Jesus himself is pictured as the leader of the army that destroys the armies of the earth in the final chapters of the book. Much blood is shed, and the birds eat the unburied bodies of the fallen warriors. After the battle there is a judgment and then re-creation can begin. Chapter 21 details the new heavens and the new earth. The vision of St. John is one of peace, security, justice, and love. Jesus says, "See, I am making all things new." The shattering effects of war give way to healing and peace, not long after the trauma and destruction.

In contrast to some of our contemporary thoughts of war, our ancient Scriptures present war without too much moral judgment. God initiates war, Jesus leads armies, and ancient people of Israel were encouraged by their leaders and by Yahweh to wage war with their neighbors. Admittedly, some of this is metaphor, some of it re-created history, but they accurately reflect the grim realities of war that were happening around them all the time. They reflect it in such a way that the post-traumatic reader will find familiar and sensible. The post-traumatic reading of Scripture will take us places we may not expect to go, with the hope for re-creation, redemption, and reconciliation.

Early Church Fathers and the Shattering Effects of War

Homicide in war is not reckoned by our Fathers as homicide...
Perhaps, however, it is well to counsel that those whose hands are
not clean only abstain from communion for three years.

—St. Basil the Great

Like the authors of the New Testament, many of the early church fathers lived during the *Pax Romana*. But the relative security of the Roman world did not make the early Church immune from persecution and what Eusebius (263–339 CE), an early historian of the Church, called "the destruction of the churches." The cruel Roman emperor Diocletian instigated one such persecution and the Church went underground to avoid further bloodshed. While describing this persecution, Eusebius quotes Lamentations 2:1–2 to indicate this persecution was the deserved judgment of God for the sloth and dissention in the churches. The passage from Lamentations describes how Yahweh destroyed the fortresses of Jerusalem and used his sword to deal out destruction and judgment. Eusebius goes on to describe in detail the martyrs who heroically endured the "deserved" persecution. After the accounts of the martyrs, in Chapter 16 of Book 8, Eusebus points out the "Change of Affairs for the Better." The division and sloth he pointed out in the churches were cured and eliminated. The Church that emerges from the shattering effects of the destruction is pure and holy. Eusebius is typical of how many early Church fathers wrote about the shattering effects of war and persecution, as well as the post-traumatic growth that followed.

Many of the fathers focus on the sin in their present age, and how judgment purified that sin. The greatest of these was Augustine of Hippo. He bridged the gap between the *Pax Romana* and the Middle Ages. He lived through the fall of Rome, and his book, *City of God,* set the theological agenda for Medieval Christendom. He wrote a considerable amount about war, and especially commented on the ethics of war. He has become the primary apologist for *jus ad bellum,* or justice in war. With his deep understanding of the human experience and failings, he wrote eloquently about war: "Let those who have read their history remember how long were the wars waged by Rome in times past, and with what diverse fortunes and grievous disasters they were attended; for the world is liable to be tempest-tossed by such misfortunes, like a storm-swept sea." Augustine likens the shattering effects of war to a storm at sea. Ships are wrecked in storms, and human lives and communities are wrecked in wars. Anyone who experiences or studies war must come to the conclusions of Augustine, that is, that war is long and disastrous, and that the world is liable to war. War cannot be excused, but it is hardly an unusual event for Augustine. It is clear from his biography that he never participated in one. According to Robert Meagher in his *Killing from the Inside Out: Moral Injury and Just War,* his views on war hint that war can be done dispassionately, without blood lust or rage. If he had been in a war, I assure you, we would be in possession of a fifteen-hundred-year-old classic about war on par with his monumental *Confessions.*

Protestant Reformers and the Shattering Effects of War

*What the proverb says is true: "War is pleasant to those who have
not experienced it." For young folk—who still have young, hot
blood—consider nothing finer than the glory and the victory of
war, by which they can shine. These carnal inclinations are easily
extinguished later on, when such folk have experienced their own
and their relatives' calamity. But before these calamities strike, the
world is ignorant of the blessings of peace, and war truly is pleasant
to those who have never experienced it. Histories show this. In them
seditious people often denounce peace. Since men usually become
sluggish and coward in times of quiet, they desire war as a sowing
for glory and an opportunity for showing their courage.*
                                                    —Martin Luther

The human fascination with war and its destructive force on the world
were well understood by Martin Luther. Ed Tick writes that "we
crave war" because it takes us to a place where we can engage life on a
mythic level. For Luther, war is spiritual because it is the result of our
"carnal inclinations." Although Luther was never a soldier himself, he was
a principal actor in the events surrounding the Peasant's Revolt in 1525.

The violence of the peasants and the subsequent reaction of the nobility produced around 100,000 deaths. It was the largest mass movement in Europe before the French Revolution. Luther refused to join with the radical peasants, choosing instead to support the nobility. Moreover, he wrote several treatises against the peasants and their leaders that called on their destruction by the secular authorities. In his *Against the Robbing and Murdering Hordes of Peasants,* Luther declares that those who die killing the rebels should be considered martyrs. The last line of the work states, "If anyone think this too hard, let him remember that rebellion is intolerable and that the destruction of the world is to be expected every hour."

Luther lived under a cloud of apocalyptic destruction and lacked insight into how war destroys the noncombatants, just as it destroys the combatants. Without firsthand knowledge of war, without knowing the post-traumatic God, it is difficult to speak to the violence in the world around us. Veterans who have participated in war need to be listened to during difficult times of national and community insecurity. Without their voices, the Church tends to rubberstamp military action or retreat altogether into an unrealistic pacifism.

During my reading of the reformers, I discovered that Ulrich Zwingli served as a military chaplain. As a young priest in sixteenth-century Switzerland, he travelled with his parishioners to the Italian peninsula where they served as mercenaries. He was their chaplain on three separate campaigns, and his first writings where treatises opposing Swiss mercenary service in Italy. He had clearly seen too much to continue to bless this system that enriched certain Swiss citizens while traumatizing others.

Even after launching the Reformation in Switzerland, forsaking his office as a Roman Catholic priest, and becoming a reformed pastor in Zurich, Zwingli was a thoroughly political pastor. He organized an invasion force against a neighboring Catholic Canton in retaliation for their execution of a Protestant pastor. He died in battle defending the city of Zurich against an overwhelming force of invading Roman Catholic Austrians in October 1531.

In contrast to his earlier expeditions with the Swiss mercenaries as a non-combatant chaplain, in the final battle of his life, Zwingli fought and died with his sword in his hand. From a contemporary perspective there are many things to criticize in the life of Zwingli. Perhaps his greatest legacy is his influence on the Cantons of Switzerland, which provided a safe haven for a young French reformer named John Calvin.

Since war was an ever-present reality in Calvin's Geneva, he addressed the issue in his sermons and writing. He wrote that even the most just war soiled the participants, and those who resorted to the use of arms should do so with regret since all war is rooted in human malice. This perspective on war was more in line with the medieval Roman Catholic view that demanded penance after war. This view is being reexamined in our current discussion of moral injury, a tribute to Calvin's influence on western Protestant thought.

Whatever his shortcomings, Chaplain Zwingli was aware that the first casualty in war is always truth:

> If a foreign soldier violently bursts in, ravages your fields and vine-yards, carries off your cattle, puts your magistrates under arrest, kills your sons who stand up to defend you, violates your daughters, kicks your wife to get rid of her, murders your old servant hiding him-self in the granary, has no consideration for your supplications, and finally sets your house on fire, you think that earth ought to open and swallow him up and you ask yourself if God really exists. . . . But if you are doing the same thing to other people, you say: "Such is war!"

Zwingli's experience in combat kept him from sugarcoating the "right-ness" of only one side in conflict. This hints to me he knew something of the post-traumatic God.

Anglicans, like myself, have been involved in warfare for as long as our priests and bishops counseled the kings and queens of England (as well as their Dukes and Lords that tried to overthrow them). They accompanied troops into battle and cared for the wounded. Our greatest reformer, Thomas Cranmer, even rode out to battle in 1545 when a hostile French fleet was in full sail for Dover. At five o'clock in the morning, the archbishop was in his "privy coat with his dagger at his saddle bow" even as his page carried his helmet and hunting gun. His biographer, Diarmaid

MacCulloch, notes that this display of martial prowess may have done more for his popularity than the past decade of evangelical sermons!

The English Reformation supported the Protestant monarch of England, and they were constantly at war with France and others. Article 37 of the 39 Articles of Religion states, "It is lawful for Christian men at the commandment of the Magistrate to wear weapons and serve in the wars." This countered the pacifism of the Anabaptists and radical reformers as well as those Englishmen who were inclined toward rebellion against the king.

But this is not to say that the English reformers did not understand the shattering effects of war. In the second version of the Great Litany in 1549 the whole Church prayed, "From lightning and tempest, from plage, pestilence, and famine, from battaile and murther, and from sodain death: Good lorde deliver us." The commoners of the realm suffered the most and should pray the hardest for peace.

English Christians were expected to kill and die in the nation's wars. They did, and still do, with Church of England chaplains at their side. The crest of the British Chaplain Corps, which is almost entirely Anglican, is a cross with the Latin phrase, *"In hoc signa vinces."* These are the words spoken to a young Roman general named Constantine at the Milvan Bridge. A symbol of Christ, or maybe the cross, appeared in the sky and told him, "By this sign conquer." Conquer he did and Christendom was born.

Chaplains with this crest on their uniforms suffered and died along with thousands of young English people in World War I and World War II, as well as others before and since. English veterans have dealt with combat trauma and the trials of homecoming from the war on terror in Afghanistan and Iraq. Today, Prince Harry, himself a veteran of Iraq and Afghanistan, gives his time to charities that focus on healing the visible and invisible wounds of war.

Religious institutions have always had to struggle to know how to respond to the reality of war. They can never be entirely neutral or aloof. Everyone who experiences war knows both its seductive power and the devastation it always causes in body, mind, and spirit. The disconnection war creates has changed little since the days of Cain and Abel.

Paul Tillich and the
Shattering Effects of War

*As a first rule of thumb, therefore, you can tell a true war story by
its absolute and uncompromising allegiance to obscenity and evil.*
—Tim O'Brien in *The Things They Carried*

Paul Tillich helped me find the post-traumatic God. He experienced
the shattering effects of war like few other theologians before or
after him. His war was World War I, the war that gave us the term
"shell shocked." Throughout this book I will return again and again to
Tillich's biography and theological work in hope that combat veterans
can find some "biographic kinship" with him. It is my contention that
Tillich's theology offers us a concept of God that can take into account
the upside-down moral universe of war.

Jonathan Shay, a psychiatrist working with Vietnam veterans in
the 1990s, wrote the classic *Achilles in Vietnam: Combat Trauma and the
Undoing of Character* and *Odysseus in America: Combat Trauma and the
Trials of Homecoming*. These books were born out of his re-reading *The
Iliad* and *The Odyssey* while convalescing in a hospital bed. He noticed
how many of the ancient warriors' speeches were similar to statements he

was hearing from his Vietnam veterans. These books show how little war trauma has changed in the last twenty-seven-hundred years.

Shay points out that the trauma of combat will produce symptoms in people. "Persistent expectation of betrayal and exploitation; destruction of the capacity for social trust, sociality, despair, isolation, and meaningless-ness." If untreated, these symptoms will "devastate life and incapacitate its victims from participation" with others. Combat trauma "shatters a sense of the fullness of the self, of the world, and of the connection between the two." Shay uses the word "shatter" to describe both the experiences of ancient and contemporary warriors.

I experienced this shattering during my year in Baghdad, Iraq. After an IED attack on an armored vehicle, I was called over to do a critical inci-dent stress management (CISM) debriefing for the survivors. Several had been killed in the attack. I was accompanied by Major Thomas Jarrett, a psychologist serving as a combat stress team provider in theater. I was glad he was there with me to help these young men with their spiritual and emotional first aid.

In an email interview with Nancy Sherman, Jarrett wrote that when a soldier experiences combat trauma, "it shatters your assumptions." There is that word again. War shatters assumptions. In its aftermath it can change a person's identity and can shatter the relationship with the self, with others, and with God. A person with a shattered, changed identity needs healing, but what is healing and how can we know if it has happened?

No one doubts that veterans who are experiencing combat trauma and the trials of homecoming need healing. We hear this word often, but rarely hear it defined. Definitions abound in the literature.

Healing is a complex psychological and theological concept that defies easy definition. Most of the books that address the needs of veterans describe in great detail the symptoms of PTSD and the common negative behaviors of people returning from combat. Less time is spent on showing what healing looks like. Healing for many is simply symptom reduction or doing the opposite of the negative behaviors.

The practical book, *Souls Under Siege: The Effects of Multiple Troop Deployments and How to Weather the Storm* by Barbara Cantrell, focuses on the strain war places on marriages. For Cantrell, the effects of war create distrust in a relationship and a lack of quality communication between couples. Therefore, healing is defined as a relationship with a higher quality of communication and a higher level of trust.

Larry Dewey, mentioned earlier, defines healing for combat veterans with PTSD as being capable of mercy, reparative acts, and forgiveness. Dewey argues that war dehumanizes the combatants—and acts of mercy, reparative acts, and forgiveness allow a person to experience the best traits of humanity after they have seen the worst traits of humanity. He concludes by pointing to *spiritual connection* as a sign of internal, spiritual healing after combat. Private and public acts of devotion indicate a connection to God. Productive work and stable marriages indicate a healthy connection to others. Healing, for Dewey, will always come from love and result in love: love for God and others.

A more comprehensive treatment of particularly Christian healing is found in the work of Episcopal priest and Jungian analyst, Morton T. Kelsey. In *Psychology, Medicine & Christian Healing,* he traces the development of Christian healing through the Hebrew Bible to the present day. Kelsey sees Jesus as a unique healer in the history of Israel. In the numerous references to miracles of healing, Kelsey sees little distinction between the mental and physical maladies in the stories. Rather, he sees Jesus responding to their needs out of love. Like Plato before him, Kelsey sees a strong link between the physical body and the emotional, mental, and spiritual life of a person. Healing must address the whole person, mind, soul, and body. Christian healing is the restoration of physical and emotional health after a divine intervention. For Kelsey, it is usually tied to the actions of the Church, often with a specific prayer or liturgy. It does not always have to be dramatic, but it must always restore the whole person to the community in mind, soul, and body.

As I read the New Testament's accounts of healings, I see physical healings as signs pointing to spiritual and communal healing, namely the forgiveness of sins. In Luke 5:23, Jesus asks whether it is easier to forgive a person's sins or say "rise up and walk!" In this story the physical healing of the man's paralysis was almost an afterthought, done only to prove the larger point that Jesus could forgive the man's sins. In spite of Jesus's emphasis on the forgiveness of sins, the people in this story are amazed by the things they saw with their eyes. It seems that no matter how much emphasis Jesus placed on the spiritual priority of healing, the crowds merely wanted a magic show.

While many veterans organizations today claim to heal veterans, the reality is more complex. Symptom replacement can be measured, but the forgiveness of sins is more difficult to quantify. It is my hope that our Church can become a place of healing for veterans.

I often wonder if Paul Tillich ever found healing after the horrors of World War I. I am only left with the evidence of his life. During the bloody campaigns in France, Tillich was hospitalized three times because of combat stress. Tillich wrote in his journal, "The impact of mass burials, without caskets, one next to the other, disfigured and covered with tent canvas and grave diggers as the only company, was dramatic and sobering. You could not help being moved by this, especially when it happened three times a day. I suspect that it would eventually destroy a person's inner contentment." This, writes Don Arther, became ominously prophetic in the years to come.

After Tillich's death, Mutie Tillich, his daughter, remembered her father's nightmares that would wake everyone in their apartment. After reading a list of PTSD symptoms, she was sure he would have been diagnosed with the disorder if he had been seen by a psychiatrist today. There is no documentary evidence in his biographies that these nightmares ever ceased.

During the war Tillich searched for healing. As the casualties mounted and were buried in mass graves, Tillich turned to his collection of art books he bought in a military bookstore. During the early days of the war, his tiny art "collection" was merely an escape. By the end of the war, it had become vastly more important to him. Tillich's search for relief from the shattering effects of war was mainly through the visual arts.

Tillich also searched for healing through psychoanalysis, which was in its infancy in the post-war years. Tillich told his biographer, "I was a barbarian when I returned from the war until a friend introduced me to a few psychoanalytic tricks of living." Whether Tillich told the analyst stories of his mother or stories of war we will never know. What we do know is that Tillich never spoke openly or at length about the war with anyone but Don Arther, himself an Air Force Chaplain. They spoke in 1964, a year before Tillich's death.

Tillich searched for healing through art, psychoanalysis, and through his work as a theologian. In spite of internal and external pressure to abandon theology for philosophy, he never bowed to the pressure. Theology, for Tillich, was a burden and a blessing. Theology allowed Tillich to express his deepest feelings about God, humanity, and the world situation. He expressed these thoughts in his lectures, which he approached with "fear and trembling" but delivered with ecstatic joy. His work was often his "ultimate concern" and he pursued it to the neglect of almost every other relationship.

I am not sure if he found holistic healing in this world, and, if not, I hope he found it in the world to come. What I do know, however, is that he helped others find it. One of his best-known sayings was, "You are accepted." He urged his readers and listeners to have the courage to accept the acceptance of God's love. In a letter to a friend he said, "Yes, I have produced the phrase 'You are accepted,' but I can never say it to *me*."

In his last furlough during World War I, Tillich had an experience as he stood in front of Botticelli's "Madonna with Singing Angels" in Berlin. He was filled with wonder and awe. He was, in words he often used, "grasped" by the absolute. The "absolute" was an expression Tillich used to describe God as the absolute ground of being. This concept will be described in greater detail later in the book. Healing, for Tillich, was being grasped by the absolute, that is, by God.

Transcendent experiences during war are nothing new and are not restricted to time and place. Karl Marlantes, in his book about his Vietnam experiences entitled, *What It Is Like to Go to War,* asks the reader to consider that "[m]ystical or religious experiences have four common components: constant awareness of one's own inevitable death, total focus on the present moment, the valuing of other people's life above one's own, and being part of a larger religious community." Every one of these four exists in combat. "The big difference is that the mystic sees heaven and the warrior sees hell."

One of the soldiers I deployed with was very mystical and quite different from most of the other enlisted soldiers he served with. Before we deployed, he called me to come over to his house to perform an exorcism on a wooden cabinet. In the wood grain of the cabinet's face he had been seeing a demon's face. It had been disturbing his wife and children, as much as it disturbed him. I could not see any face in the wood grain, but I prayed for his family as they prepared for deployment.

He would often confide in me about the demons that were present in our area. He told me the whole area was under an evil power. It was hard to argue with him from the middle of Baghdad. He gave me a ring with a Star of David on it to ward off the evil spirits. I still have the ring and think of him, remember his words, "It [evil] is over there and coming this way." He was always pointing to the west. There were times when I knew he was right. After all, when we renounce Satan in our baptismal liturgy we face the west. When we "Turn to Jesus Christ" we turn and face east. I could see destruction all around me. It was more than just the destruction of the war, it was like the whole world was descending into chaos and we were all on the brink of ruin. Many soldiers in my area attempted suicide, and some completed it. Self-destruction seems to be the hallmark of demonic activity in the four Gospels. Is it any wonder I would see so much of it in Iraq?

When this would overwhelm me, I would look at that ring. It was beautiful, silver and turquoise, likely of Middle Eastern origin, forged in a place where visual symbols had a closer connection to the thing they symbolized.

Six years after I returned from Iraq, I met and married my wife, Sarah. She is an accomplished art historian and museum curator specializing in contemporary art. Living with her and accompanying her to art openings around the world has opened my eyes to the transcendent possibilities of art for healing. Art does not work quickly, I have found. It needs a relationship to flourish. Art needs time to change consciousness. Four years later, I know it has changed me for the better.

On the psych ward at Walter Reed, a dedicated art therapist named Melissa Walker opened patients' eyes to the transformative possibilities of making art. Her work with veterans expanded to a wider audience when *National Geographic* published many of her patients' masks in February 2015. It is difficult to prove how art transforms the soul, but those who have been gripped by its gentle power know the truth.

Paul Tillich and the Trials of Homecoming

War is the foyer to hell; coming home is hell.
—Tyler Boudreau in *Packing Inferno: the Unmaking of a Marine*

Paul Tillich's post-war, post-traumatic life was relationally tumultuous and unorthodox. The normal pre-war rules seemed to no longer apply to him. This mild-mannered boy was raised in a Germany that mirrored, in many ways, Victorian society in England with its strict moral codes and well-defined courtship rituals. When Tillich came home from the war, the world he left had changed. Germany was a defeated nation and the old codes and morals no longer held sway, especially for the generation who fought in the war. In the environment he became, in his own words, a wild man.

When Tillich was finally discharged from the army, he returned home to discover his wife, Goethe, was pregnant with his friend's child. They soon divorced and Tillich was left with an apartment that was soon nicknamed the *Katastrophen-Diele,* the Disaster Bar. For the next five years this apartment witnessed an abortion, the birth of a baby, and a brutal robbery. Soon, the apartment became a haven for struggling artists and students. During this time Tillich experienced a "multiplicity of erotic relationships" that left him with "manifold fears, expectations, ecstasies, and despairs." It was a time of chaos and searching.

Five years after the war was over, he met Hannah Werner and married her. Paul and Hannah entered marriage with the mutual understanding, theirs would be an open marriage. Both of them had multiple affairs throughout their lifelong union. Most of the information about these liaisons comes from the book Hannah published five years after his death, *From Time to Time.* Not only does it document her husband's numerous affairs as well as a few of her own, it also depicts her walking into the room while he is watching pornography on a small home-made film screen. As images of naked women appear on the screen, all of them tied to crosses while being whipped by other naked women, she says, "So fitting for a Christian and a theologian." As one can imagine, a torrent of magazine articles about the Tillich's unconventional marriage flashed on the national media.

Hannah does not only give account of his sexual issues, she also gives account of his wartime service in the book. She writes, "Compassion came to him during the First World War, when he participated in death on the battlefield. . . . There he experienced no hostility. He broke his nationalistic ties and became a citizen of the world. He met brothers of the mind in every country and transgressed every borderline of spirit and soul."

Hannah is a poet, so she can grasp the post-traumatic God better than the theologian. Deep compassion for the world, coupled with an erosion of borders and categories, is how she described him. This movement of the spirit is deep and disturbing, especially when it crosses the borders of human sexual norms like monogamy or exploitation.

The danger of the post-traumatic God is found in this transgression of borders, just as salvation is found in transgressing borders. Jesus certainly did this, living as he was under the shadow of his own impending death. He crossed borders—geographic, cultural, and moral—to send a message to humanity about the deeper essence of God. Jungian analyst and Episcopal priest J. Pittman McGehee is fond of pointing out, "The sacred breaking into the profane." The sacred story of Christianity is found, McGehee writes in *The Invisible Church,* in a profane structure. Finding transcendence in immanence is a profound challenge and quest of the spiritual life. Tillich was definitely on that quest, although the quest took him to dangerous and hurtful places at times.

Some of the edge of Hannah's book is blunted by Rollo May's *Paulus: Tillich as Spiritual Teacher.* The book followed Hannah's and served as a sort of rebuttal to her claims of infidelity. As Tillich's closest friend and one-time student, a disciple if there ever was one, May explains how Tillich loved people and was intimate with women, but rarely crossed sexual lines. Separating fact from fiction in Tillich's sex life is as difficult as separating fact from fiction in any historical character's biography. However, we can be certain his sex life was not monogamous while he was married to Hannah.

In spite of his numerous professional achievements, his familial relationships continued to suffer. Open marriages, after all, are hardly open from one spouse to the other. There are too many long absences and silences. I focus on Paul Tillich's sex life here because I believe his dysfunction is linked to his experience as a combat veteran.

Most combat veterans have strict expectation and rituals concerning sexual relationships; when these rules are broken, a period of chaos ensues. In fact, Tillich himself linked his combat experience to the pursuit of the erotic. Writing about the wild days in post-war Germany, he said, "I have come to know the *Boheme;* I went through the war."

Jonathan Shay in his *Odysseus in America* provocatively writes about how soldiers, like Odysseus, are seduced, drowned, and betrayed by sirens and goddesses on their journey home from war. The combat veteran's hatred and disrespect of women is turned into patterns of infidelity and dishonesty, all of which were embodied in Tillich during the post-war years.

Several combat chaplains I interviewed for my doctoral project spoke of their increased sexual appetite. This surprised them, especially after encountering traumatic situations involving death and dying. Procreation is, after all, the only way we can physically and practically attempt to reverse our losses in death. During one group interview, these same chaplains asked the one female observer to leave the room so they could be candid about their experience. This indicated to me the shame that comes from talking about "abnormal" sexual desires and fantasies. The relationship between abnormal sexual experiences and shame is a close one, and one that ministers to veterans must pay close attention to.

For me, my time in Iraq disconnected me from the feminine. Even though I served with many women and was myself a non-combatant, the hyper-masculine nature of war and military service seeped into my soul. I functioned out of this energy when I returned. I was obsessed with strength and threat. I saw threats around me and attempted to be one myself at times. I was drawn to women, but I despised them as they fell from the high pedestal I had constructed for them.

· Karl Marlantes shows how warriors must get back in touch with their own feminine energy after war. He did it by drinking tea with women out of fine china while he was studying abroad. Being reunited with the feminine is the ultimate homecoming that veterans long for. Because of my shattered marriage, there was little home for me to come home to. I know from the thousands of warriors I have counseled that I am not alone in this. My relentless pursuit of sex and relationships, some of which were chronicled in my memoir, *Death Letter: God, Sex, and War,* were attempts to find a home.

Ed Tick is more philosophical about sex by pointing out that when we call upon the god of war Ares, the goddess of lust Aphrodite shows up. The god of war and the goddess of lust have a way of finding each other in combat or after homecoming. The sexual relationships combat veterans have are often unorthodox or unacceptable to conventional society. Tillich's experience is congruent with the shattering of relationships and societal conventions that combat veterans experience.

Tillich's experience shares some similarities with the ever-popular Christian writer, C. S. Lewis. While a student at Oxford, Lewis joined the army, just as many young Oxford men while World War I raged in Europe. He was wounded by a "friendly" artillery shell and evacuated to a hospital in the rear, then released.

Sometime after his hospitalization he began a relationship with Janie Moore. Moore was the mother of his close friend who died in the war. She was forty-six and separated from her husband. Lewis was twenty-one. So began an unconventional relationship, to say the least. He called her "Mother" in public, even as they maintained a sexual relationship for many years. In effect, she was his common law wife for more than thirty years. As he approached middle age and she her elderly years, their relationship changed. She suffered from dementia and was often hostile to him. He visited her every day until the day she died.

I share this here because Lewis never talked or wrote about two things, trench warfare in World War I or his intimate and loving relationship with Janie Moore. One can hardly blame him for his silence about either. His short extremely shallow treatment of both subjects in his autobiography, written four years after Moore's death, makes his readers poorer for it.

His only writing about the war is his poetry, published in his first and only book of poetry. One of his haunting lines about the trenches shows the reader who he had become.

> What call have I to dream of anything?
> I am a wolf. Back to the world again,
> And speech of fellow-brutes that once were men
> Our throats can bark for slaughter: cannot sing.

A few years after my time in Iraq, I sat anxiously in a waiting room of the social work department of Walter Reed. I was about to attend a session with a licensed counselor. I had been in plenty of counseling sessions, but this time I was the client, the patient. This time it was for me. I wondered if one of my colleagues or superiors would walk in and see me reading a magazine, the reason for my presence all too obvious.

Finally, I was called into one of the offices. The social worker asked me the dozens of intake questions. I told her I had been having anxiety and sadness since my divorce. "What happened?" she asked. I said my wife cheated on me and we divorced. "How long ago." I thought back to the hazy past. I knew it had been over a year, but normal time was not working for me anymore. I was jumping around in time, it seemed. I was an adolescent one minute, an old man the next. I could see the moment of my birth and I could feel the coffin lid close over me. I was surviving. Life was surreal, a common expression for the traumatized. I never could be fully present for anything during those days. I was like a shark, always fidgeting, always on the move.

The survival energy I developed in Iraq had not left me. I was the predator and the prey. I was always hunting, always the hunted.

"How long ago was your divorce?" she asked again. "Eleven months," I said, snapping out of my time travel. She probed more. "Why did you divorce again?" "Um, yeah, she had a boyfriend when I got back from Iraq, in '06." I did not tell her about what I had done and what I had left undone. I did not say how numb I was when I got home. I did not mention how self-obsessed I was with my own success as an army chaplain. I did not tell her how little respect I showed my ex-wife.

"So, you were cuckolded," the social worker said. "I can see how that would be hard to take." I had heard that word before, but never applied it to me. "Yeah, I was, I guess," was my feeble reply. It is hard to take on a label in life. This was the first of many I would end up with. They are very difficult at first, but grow easier with time. I never wanted to be divorced. I never wanted to be a veteran either. I never wanted to be defined by something in my past—that is why I kept all the rules! I certainly did not want to be a cuckold.

A cuckold is a man whose wife is cheating on him. Some of them know it is happening, some do not. It is an old term, just as it is an old situation. It goes all the way back to the Roman legionnaires. They would march back into town, bedecked with horned helmets given to them for success in battle. After years of being away, they would often discover their wives and lovers had been unfaithful. The horns of success became symbols of failure in fidelity. Being good at fighting does not equal success in relationships. It is an old problem; it is not just Paul Tillich and myself that bear this name.

Sometimes men do the cheating. I have heard their confessions, the admissions of guilt. After hearing many of these, I can confidently say I would rather be the one cheated upon than the one doing the cheating. Cuckolds only have to lie to themselves, never to their spouse, and there is some comfort in this.

Military chaplains, just like other veterans, experience all the shattering and disconnecting effects of war. War shatters their connection to their pre-traumatic identity. This can be alarming for a group of clergy who pride themselves in our ability to cultivate relationships.

One of the earliest, honest accounts of a chaplain's difficult journey home from war is Roger Benimoff's *Faith Under Fire: An Army Chaplain's Memoir*. Benimoff's experience with PTSD prompted him to pen in his journal, "I am angry at God for putting me in a helpless situation." Later in the account he writes about his estrangement from his wife that almost results in divorce. He says, "I still believed in God, but not necessarily a compassionate one." His own son once asked his mother, "Is that why Daddy doesn't care about us anymore?" I am thankful Benimoff was brave enough to tell us his story of his problems with God.

His problems with God center around God's compassion. For some, the post-traumatic God is not compassionate. If God were compassionate, then God would have done something about the suffering I witnessed. Civilians can believe in a compassionate God from the safety of their suburbs and apartments, but those who have witnessed the indifference of war know that God is not just a bubbling fountain of melted chocolate. God is not a big muffin in the sky from whom we all can take a bite, or not. No, the God often revealed in war is cruel, vengeful, killing the good and the young and leaving the corrupt and the evil to flourish. It is the deepest and most personal of all theological questions. It is the subject of books, songs, psalms, and groans in the night.

A Vietnam veteran shared in one of our Episcopal Veterans Fellowship meetings that he had "put God on the shelf" during Vietnam. Stories of

God's disappearance in war abound. God went AWOL (absent without leave) over there. I had those feelings after Iraq. God was supposed to send me to Iraq to have great success. I would serve the troops, preach great sermons, and counsel troubled souls. I would return to great fanfare and love. I would move on with my life and live a life of happiness and wedded bliss. None of this happened. I was an anxiety-ridden, angry, flighty, depressed, and alcoholic-dependent man. I was not able to enjoy anything, even time with my two young sons. I was obsessed with my own safety, and a string of ex-girlfriends proved my lack of commitment. All I could think of was myself, in a primitive ego-centrism. I was filled with shame over my divorce and avoided married people. I did not trust anyone unless they served with me in Iraq. I pushed friends and family away and I was angry at God.

"War is the father of all," said the fifth-century BCE philosopher Heraclites. I participated in war, and the war participated in me. War became my father, not God. War offered me the chance to be a man, to grow up, to make my mark on the world. The god of war, traditionally the Roman Mars, equivalent to the Greek Ares, is showy, fickle, and rash. I was more like him than I knew. We live and move in our mythology and I was deep in this one.

It was during these days that I discovered Paul Tillich. I do not know how I stumbled upon the hidden (to me) historical fact that he was an army chaplain in World War I. I read his theology and found a post-traumatic God I could believe in.

There are three major themes in Paul Tillich's thought that helped me during those days. I believe these three concepts can help post-traumatic pilgrims, veterans who have been to hell and back, because they were developed by a theologian whose theology was, according to his own words, "completed" by his experience in combat. Tillich's three theological themes are: the courage to be, the new being, and God as the ground of being.

The Courage to Be

In the world you will face persecution. But take courage;
I have overcome the world.

—Jesus, John 16:33

William James, in his classic *The Varieties of Religious Experience,* devotes a chapter to "The Divided Self: And the Process of Its Unification." Human beings often feel at odds with themselves, especially after war. Craig Mullaney described the feeling in his Iraq memoir, *The Unforgiving Minute: A Soldier's Education.* He described this feeling as being "dislocated." After learning of his father's affair while deployed, he entered the half-lit world of the alcoholic. Questions about his own character assaulted his mind and he summed this period up by saying, "I wasn't the me I was before." The combat-tested warrior cannot recognize himself in the mirror.

Henry Knox Sherrill was a chaplain in the U.S. Army during World War I. The young Episcopal priest served in a field hospital full of wounded and dying men who came to him directly from the trenches. Many years later, after serving as presiding bishop of the Episcopal Church (1947–1958), he wrote in his autobiography that, upon his return to the states, his mother said he "had grown hard." What she fully meant we shall never know. What we do know is enough. We know how the succession of dying young men might have created a deep callous on his soul. We know how we grow accustomed to the wounds of war. Severed legs and arms, all witnessing to the power of weapons most Americans will never hear with their own ears. I know some of this from my time in an army hospital. The numbers of wounded young women and men seemed to be legion at times. They seemed to be everywhere. If I saw someone walking toward me, I would be surprised if they did not have a prosthetic limb.

During the days when the details of my wife's affair were coming to light, I grew so nauseous I could barely eat. In contrast to my normal, big army lunches, the best I could do was nibble half of a Jr. Whataburger. I went from a healthy 180 pounds to around 155 in a matter of weeks. By the time I started at Walter Reed, about four months later, I developed an obsession with running. I would run ten to twenty miles every day. Twice a week I would run a twenty-six-mile loop around the Washington Monument. I was searching for something to control in a world that had suddenly spun out of control.

As the nausea diminished, I developed an obsession with staying thin, and disordered eating followed. I developed a familiar rhythm to deal with my anxiety. First, I would run. If I could not run because I was injured or had already run, I would drink beer. If I could not drink because I was on duty or visiting my tee-totaling parents, I would binge eat.

There were times during my night shifts at the hospital where I would take a break from responding to emergencies by eating box after box of Girl Scout cookies that had been donated to the hospital. Walter Reed received these boxes of cookies by the thousands every month, and the chaplain's office always kept a well-stocked closet of them. With each bite I would despair and take another. With each bite my anxiety would diminish as the pain in my stomach grew. Sometimes I could barely get out of the chair when the pager went off for another emergency call.

The next morning I would fast, vowing never to do it again. I would run a long distance, still exhausted from the all-night shift, vowing never to do it again. All my resolutions not to drink were made after a night of drinking. All my resolutions to avoid binge eating were always made after a binge. I hated being this way. I hated myself for my weakness. I never told anyone about it except one therapist. She offered that I say "I love myself" every time I took a bite of a cookie. That worked for a while, then it did not.

My shattered relationship with myself began to heal as I explored Paul Tillich's idea of existential courage in the face of doubt. His idea is expressed in his most popular book, *The Courage to Be.* In this book Tillich explores the concept of courage. He writes that the supreme example of courage is a soldier. He knows this because he was one. Courage is the ability to look into the abyss of death, and that is to experience the threat of non-being. Non-being is another way of saying meaninglessness.

Tillich looked into the abyss of death in World War I when he listened to the moans of the wounded and saw the wasted landscape of "iron, fire, and blood." He looked into the abyss of death when he preached a sermon in a blasted church in France in 1916. He spoke to his soldiers saying, "We all [are] deeply terrified by the abyss which opened up to us." This was the existential abyss he read about in Nietzsche's *Thus Spoke Zarathustra.* He read this book in a French forest during that same bloody year.

While many of Nietzsche's ideas were embraced by Tillich, most notably his insistence that the God often portrayed by popular religion does not exist, Tillich rejected Nietzsche's self-reliance and "will to power" that was "used and abused by the Nazis."

The last line of Tillich's *The Courage to Be* is instructive and makes the rather dense book worth reading. "The courage to be is rooted in the God who appears when God disappears in the anxiety of doubt." God disappears in the abyss, in the anxiety or war or homecoming. In that anxiety we doubt and that is the opposite of courage. Doubt isolated me from others and from my true self. The angrier I became, the farther I went from anyone who tried to come close to me. How could I get close to anyone when I hated myself? Tillich's admonition to have courage in the face of death, doubt, and despair resonated with me. I wanted this courage.

Jesus said in Matthew 16:25: "For those who want to save their life will lose it, and those who lose their life for my sake will find it." Doubt tries to preserve life at any cost, even the cost of despair. Courage understands the reality of death and the threat of non-being and embraces life. For me, I found courage by embracing the forgiveness of my sins.

For Tillich, the forgiveness of sins means acceptance. As an existentialist theologian, he spent a great deal of time describing humanity's existential estrangement in the second volume of his *Systematic Theology*. From this detailed description of estrangement, he moves to describe how Jesus as the Christ conquers this human estrangement.

The four Gospels describe how Jesus conquered sin and estrangement by resisting Satan's temptations in the desert and experiencing anxiety in the garden the night before his crucifixion. For Tillich, the crucifixion and resurrection of Jesus are forever linked in a bond of interdependence. These interdependent events are both reality and symbol because they happened in time and history, but they also have a greater function in salvation. Tillich acknowledges that the New Testament places a great deal of emphasis on the objective side of these events and elevates them to universal significance. The cross and resurrection form the symbol of the unity between god and humanity that cannot be broken by the ultimate estrangement—death. The atonement is, above all, power over the enslaving structures of evil and the healing of people from their existential estrangement. The atonement reconciles God and humanity and is dependent on the merit of Christ. St. Paul's term "In Christ" is marked by "faith instead of unbelief, surrender, instead of *hubris,* and love instead of concupiscence." This is regeneration and repentance for Tillich. His thinking was very different from the interpretations of the atonement I heard as a child.

Tillich taught that when a person accepts the reality of God's acceptance through Jesus Christ, the person is then able to be "In Christ," that is, in the new being. "The objective reality of the new being precedes the subjective participation in it." God's grace comes to us before we feel it. For a traumatized person whose feelings are askew and unreliable, this would be a relief indeed.

Although Tillich emphasized the objective work of Christ that creates the possibility for humans to experience unity with God, he is better known for his emphasis on the subjective feeling of acceptance, rather than a more objective justification in heaven. He saw the phrase "justification by faith" largely responsible for the Protestant "distortion" of seeing the possibility for "self-salvation" based on knowledge of doctrine rather than being "grasped" by God in faith. The personal encounter with God and the reunion with him are the heart of all genuine religion, he said.

Personal encounters with God were the subject of much of my early faith life. I wondered how other people experienced God. I wondered what they heard or what they felt in those moments. Recently, a Vietnam veteran told me he was sitting in church on Christmas Eve when something happened to him. He told me why Christmas Eves were difficult for him. He lost eight friends one Christmas Eve in Vietnam during an intense rocket attack. The rockets hit his artillery position, a position he was supposed to be at, but at the last minute was called away from. The moral injury was palpable as he described the thirty-plus years of hating Christmas Eve. But on this particular Christmas Eve, seated there near a window of the church, he saw something out the window. Here, the man proceeded to pull out his iPad and show me a picture of the empty church sanctuary. He said, "I was sitting right there."

He said he looked out the window and noticed the light from the windows extended to the tree line. When he looked out that night, he saw all eight of his friends standing there, looking in at him through the window. He said, "You know what they said? We're OK, it's OK. That's what they said."

I had heard and felt a version of this same message "It's OK" before, on a balcony in the dark days that followed my return from Iraq and divorce. The following is an excerpt from my memoir, *Death Letter: God, Sex, and War:*

On the balcony of the apartment, I look out into the night. Cars drive by on the road below. Each one is headed somewhere. Only the parked cars lack a destination. Like Abram in the Old Testament, I look up at the sky and question the God who promised me a good marriage. I tell him I had damn near done everything I was supposed to do and now everything is a god-damn mess. My voice rises from the whisper of my mind and I speak. I yell at the Master of the Universe and tell him I didn't like what happened. I taunt him for how he turned his Almighty back on me when I needed him most. I rail on, "Don't you care that she left me? Don't you want us together?" There's nothing but silence. I know that answer, but I can't believe it. I know that God loves my ex-wife as much as he loves me. I feel most betrayed by this thought. Whose side is God on in a war? Whose side is he on in a divorce? Whose side is he on in the Super Bowl?

Then the questions break. I whimper, sob, then burst into a full-on ugly cry. I weep at the silent stars and the fingernail-shaped moon. I hope all the clocks will stop and die with my soul. When I stop weeping, I hear a voice. The voice is silence. It is the stillness of the unconditioned. It is a voice that is unconditioned, like a horse standing still. There is Kierkegaard's royal coachman seated above him with a whip, poised to strike at the slightest movement of the horse. It is the Universe or God or the Great Ground of Being herself that has a message for me. The voice says, "You can leave her now." The voice is not my own. My weeping has been heard, but God has surprised me in the worst way imaginable. I don't believe him and walk back inside.

Up until this point in my journey, I thought God wanted me to stay married at all costs. I thought God believed in the institution of marriage and was depending on me to keep it humming along. I did not know I was dealing with the post-traumatic God, a God who cares little for institutions, but does care, in some incomprehensible way, for me.

I have heard this same message a few other times in my work with veterans. I have heard them describe that feeling of peace that overwhelmed me on that dark night. It seems to resonate with people in crisis. It is, after all, what we say to the dying and the wounded, "It's OK," even when it is clearly not OK. These are the words we whisper to our children when they cry and, apparently, sometimes, the words the post-traumatic God whispers to us.

In contrast to Tillich's description of the forgiveness of sins as existential acceptance, Tillich's contemporary in Switzerland, Karl Barth, emphasized the eschatological nature of our salvation in Jesus Christ. In his sermon, "Saved by Grace," Barth says, "To be saved does not just mean to be a little encouraged, a little comforted, a little relieved. It means to be pulled out like a log from a burning fire." Barth describes how unaware people are of their sinfulness and how they are on "thin ice" in regard to destruction and judgment. He is like his spiritual forefather, Jonathan Edwards, who illustrated a sinner walking on a rotting canvas in his famous sermon, "Sinners in the Hands of an Angry God." Barth describes humanity walking across a frozen lake at night, unaware they on a lake at all. At any moment the ice can break and we will be in the eternal judgment.

Barth's version of salvation is more like what I heard as a child. You can see how a new approach to these concepts could give me a new vision of my own salvation and the salvation of the world. Tillich's theology certainly grasped me at the right time. I was finding theism hard to believe. At least I found the theism of my childhood hard to believe. As I reflect on these theologically tumultuous days, I have come to the conclusion we may need different theology in order to handle the present trauma of our lives. This does not mean that this particular theological view will last forever. Like a tourniquet, it may stop the blood flow for a while, thus saving the limb. I certainly needed a different theology during those first post-traumatic years.

I wonder if this was what happened to English mathematician turned philosopher Alfred North Whitehead. While working in London as an academic mathematician, Whitehead's son Eric was killed in Tillich's war, World War I, while serving in the Royal Air Force. Shortly after his son's death, Whitehead turned from mathematics and began to work on philosophical problems. Very little is known of Whitehead's motives at this turning point in his life due to the intense privacy he maintained throughout his life and the fact that his papers were destroyed by his wife after his death in 1947. My thoughts here are purely speculative. What I do know is that the loss of a teenager in war has a profound effect on parents. I have seen it with my own eyes.

At Seminary of the Southwest in Austin, Texas, I took an elective course in Process Thought and read Whitehead's *Process and Reality,* all the while thinking of the writer's grief for his son lost in war. Was this the philosophical problem that changed his life's course? Who can know? It is amazing what the mind can do when confronted with a problem. Whitehead's problem was as old as Job: How could this happen to me if there is a God in control of the universe? God, for Whitehead, changed. The God he describes at the final climax of his difficult and confusing (for me and many others) book is not conditioned by the normal theological rules Christianity has often confessed.

He rejects the Aristotelian concept of God as the "unmoved mover" as well as Christianity's "eminently real" God. A transcendent creator whose will must be obeyed "is the fallacy which has infused tragedy into the histories of Christianity and of Mahometanism." I do not know the specific tragedies he is referencing, but those who were touched by World War I could not escape its theological implications. Religion, for Whitehead, is just an imitation of Caesar with all his pomp and authoritarian grandeur.

In contrast to the theological system of his day, the God in *Process and Reality* can exist in some relation to the terrible suffering in the world without being the cause of it. Even God is affected by the temporal processes of this world. I cannot explicate all of Whitehead's theological insights, but I do hope to suggest that profound loss and suffering can lead to new conceptions of God and that this is what people often need when faced with trauma.

John Cobb was an influential pioneer in early Process Theology. When answering the theological questions of a recent tragedy, the Sendai earthquake, he answers with Process Theology in order to comfort: "The suffering of the people in Sendai evokes compassion all over the world. God is present in that compassion and even where human compassion fails to reach. God is not in control, but God's love upholds us always and everywhere and especially here and now where suffering and need are most acute." We should expect post-traumatic people to find a post-traumatic theology that helps them in the moment of their greatest need.

That Tillich's understanding of salvation was different than Barth's is clear. Tillich, in his sermon "You Are Accepted," defines sin and grace for his secular, philosophically minded audience. He begins with an apology for using such archaic terms. Indeed, sin and grace are rarely used outside of religion. Among the few exceptions are chocolate desserts (sinful) and banking and dancing (grace period and smoothness on the dance floor). But Tillich insists on using these terms because no other words can convey the reality of what needed to be expressed. Indeed, even today, the subject of moral injury is simply another way to say sin. Moral injuries are the things done and left undone. They are the things we confess we have done against God and our neighbor. But for Tillich, all other substitutes are shallow. Instead of tossing the archaic terms, he seeks to rediscover their meaning in a way that explores the depth of human existence. Like Barth he affirms that all are sinners, but sin is, for Tillich, separation. This separation is separation from oneself, from others, and from the ground of being—God. This separation is universal, and the separation results in suffering.

Both Barth and Tillich are very detailed and dramatic in their descriptions of this suffering. Both point to the destructive suffering that is often self-inflicted. Tillich, however, points out that we know *why* we suffer. We suffer because we are separated and we are separated because we exist. "Existence is separation! Before sin is an act, it is a state," he wrote in *Shaking the Foundations*. For Tillich, the remedy for human estrangement is found in the experience of St. Paul on the road to Damascus. Jesus as the Christ appears to Saul, soon to be Paul. In the moment of his greatest separation, Paul found himself accepted in spite of his being rejected. Grace overwhelmed him. For Tillich, this means more than the belief God exists or that Jesus is the Savior or that the Bible contains the truth. Grace must "strike us" at the moment of our greatest despair and discouragement. "Simply accept the fact that you are accepted," he wrote. When acceptance is accepted, then reunion is possible between the separated parts of ourselves, others, and God.

Tillich's existentialist emphasis on psychological salvation gained him acceptance with many intellectuals of his day, if only for a short time. This sermon, when compared to Barth's "Saved by Grace," demonstrates the place of Jesus Christ's death in Tillich's theology. Tillich refers to Jesus three times in this sermon, in contrast to Barth's urging his hearers to "look to Jesus Christ" in almost every paragraph of the homily.

Whether there is too little of Jesus in Tillich or too much Jesus in Barth matters little to me. What does matter is a cryptic statement Barth made to Tillich that Tillich was "still fighting the Grand Inquisitor." Tillich responded many years later that Barth was right to point this out. Was this a piece of Tillich's trauma seeping out into his vision of salvation and God? Did Barth, with his keen insight into the human condition, see something disturbed beneath the dignified German theologian's persona? This exchange between these two giants of the twentieth century, in my mind, illustrates the very different perspective of Paul Tillich. This post-traumatic perspective was formed in the first and only turning point of his life, World War I.

Today, I am glad Tillich described salvation this way because it gave me, in the state I was in, an invitation to stay in fellowship with Christ and his Church. Without this link, I do not know where I would have gone. Although so many details of our lives were different, our biographic kinship around a few experiences brought me close to his words and thoughts. His words spoke to me in my post-traumatic abyss and they brought me back into God's presence. Since I met Tillich in his books, I have found more courage to live life in spite of the snagging pull of despair, doubt, and suicide. I had to take courageous steps to move towards health and community. Some of those steps were walking back into a church. The courage to be is rooted in a God who accepts us in our estrangement. I felt this acceptance in the Church that found me after war.

The New Being

I had to walk out of church when they prayed for the troops.
I wanted to think about something else.
—"George," an Army chaplain one year
after redeployment

did not feel acceptance in the Church right away after my return
from Iraq. In fact, I carried with me a huge sense of estrangement.
Tillich also felt estrangement from his Christian community when he
returned from World War I. He became especially aware of his shattered relationship with others during church services when he realized
Christians were hiding their feelings of joy and trying to pass off an
"emaciated, intentionally childish, unexciting, un-ecstatic thing, without
color or danger, without heights or depths." Tillich turned from this
lifeless community and embraced an alternate way of being. His experience resonates with many combat veterans who come back to a world
obsessed with seemingly petty issues and concerns.

One veteran described to me his anger about a conversation he over-
heard while waiting in line to order at a fast-food restaurant. Two young
women were discussing what dress they should wear to a party that evening. As they talked about colors and styles, his rage grew, disproportionate

to what he was hearing. Like the young warrior in the film *The Hurt Locker,* veterans stare down the grocery store aisle, too full of choices, and instead hear the whirring of helicopter blades.

When relationships with others are shattered post-trauma, space can open up for the new being. Citing Galatians 6:15, "For neither circumcision counts for anything nor un-circumcision, but a new creation" (RSV), Tillich introduces his concept of the new being. The new being is not circumcision. Tillich equates St. Paul's use of circumcision with the religious systems of the world. Circumcision is a religious rite that is merely external and archaic. All the great religions have rites of initiation, and circumcision represents them in all their essentially empty pomp and pretention. The new being is not so concerned with the concerns of organized religion.

But neither is the new being concerned with anti-religious thought. The idea of un-circumcision in Galatians represents the movements of fascism, communism, secular humanism, and ethical idealism. The new being is not anti-religious—it is not atheistic. Tillich argued that these secular, anti-religious movements are empty and devoid of meaning because they ignore the vast spiritual world and place their ultimate concern and faith in the finite. When the finite is elevated to the status of a god, it can easily become demonic. Tillich criticized Nazism and other totalitarian states as demonic states, since they demanded that people elevate the temporal to the level of the eternal.

Many veterans who have their faith shaken in war quickly turn to agnosticism and atheism. These are, after all, viable alternatives to believing God was AWOL during the war. Others turn to fundamentalism. Tillich, no doubt, flirted with agnosticism and atheism. He certainly read enough Nietzsche in war-torn France to make a convincing case for such a belief system. But he did not go that direction. Both fundamentalism and atheism offer us certainty, an attractive concept after war shatters our sense of right and wrong. In what universe is killing a child acceptable behavior? In war, on a convoy, it is. When we come home from this upside-down world, we can crave certainty, even if it disconnects us from the people and reality around us.

In the years after my time in Iraq, I would often have physical reactions to sights, sounds, and smells that reminded me of the God of my childhood. I realize now I was overreacting, or at least reacting out of my own pain. But a person can rarely see one's own overreaction in the moment. I avoided my parents' church as much as possible and anything that reminded me of it. I would start arguments with other Christians about their "personal" God, and this left me further estranged from the people that wanted to help me. It was during these days that I read about Tillich's concept of the new being.

The new being does not replace the old way of being but it is a renewal of the old form. Renewal and reconciliation happen when we understand how deeply we are loved and accepted. The message of the cross is the message of resurrection and reconciliation. When differences of sex, race, beauty, strength, or knowledge no longer divide humans, then we experience the new being.

Today, in the archives of the Harvard Divinity School Library, one can see the communion chalice Tillich carried with him in World War I. He kept this small metal cup with him in his office until it was eventually preserved in the collection of his books and papers. Tillich is not known for his emphasis on the specific practice of communion. However, Tillich's whole theology emphasized the sacramental reality of the person of Christ. Christ, in Tillich's thought, is the symbol that participates in the power it represents. The symbol Christ is based on the image and person of Jesus, and always points to Jesus not just as a Jewish man of the first century, but to Jesus as the Messiah and the one who redeemed humanity through his death on the cross.

The new being is Christ's body in the world, and thus a sacrament for the world because it reconciles people to each other and it reconciles humans to God. The new being is a community that is not bound by ritual or unbelief, but in the very personal presence of Jesus Christ. It lives in the boundary between religion and anti-religion. It demolishes stereotypes and stands alone. It addresses the fundamental estrangement that Tillich addressed again and again throughout his life.

Tillich's sermons tackled the existential estrangement and death that exist in the world. Tillich, an army chaplain who absorbed the horrors of combat into his theology, preaches to us from the grave that "love is stronger than death." In an era obsessed with the false promises of science, he said we need to see something stronger than death. Veterans who have been changed by their experience with death and the destructive innovations of science can embrace new life in the new being.

Tillich's concept of the new being helped me immensely in my postwar odyssey. In this concept I recognized the new community I had joined as being, in its own way, sacred and holy. The community I joined after I came home from Iraq was a blending of army and hippie culture.

I knew several divorced people in my childhood. I knew them because of the rumors that swirled around them. A person's divorce was spoken about in hushed tones, like it was a crime. It was hard for the Christians in my community to trust divorced people. I remember asking a man in my church if he was worried about divorced people stealing other people's spouses. He replied, "Well, they did once, didn't they?"

Divorced people were not allowed to serve in church leadership or teach Sunday School. They certainly were not allowed to remarry. Some said if they did, they would be committing perpetual adultery. Others, like my father, thought it only happened once. They were trying to take Jesus's words seriously. He was, after all, the most anti-divorce person in the Bible.

When I got divorced, I entered a world of shame. I was numbered among the transgressors. Because I had two boys, I could not hide it. As soon as I started speaking about my life, my kids, my job, my schedule, the divorce came up. One of the things that always bothered me about being divorced was how people pry into your life. So many people ask why I got divorced, as if I could explain it to them. Simple answers work best, but the question always carried with it some judgment. I noticed that divorced people asked this question less than people who had never been divorced. Even more often than the "Why" question, people almost always ask how often I get to see my kids. It's a strange question. No one asks married people this. I suppose if I said "Never" that would be worse than "I have sole custody." From either of these answers, or something in the middle, they could ascertain the level of shame to assign me. At least, that is what I imagined.

Now that I have been divorced for years and remarried, I have gotten used to all the questions. Sometimes I say the normal "every other weekend" or I say, depending on my annoyance level, "as much as I want to." Other times I jokingly ask them back about what day they pay their mortgage or rent. I know they mean well, but it always felt like a shame spotlight shining in on my dark, private world.

On many army forms there are three boxes to check: single, married, or divorced. Checking the divorced box was not easy at first, but it got easier. When soldiers would look at me wide-eyed with wonder saying, "You're divorced?" I would often say, "Yes, it's one of the job-related hazards."

I knew this going into my deployment to Iraq. At a military ceremony, shortly before we deployed, a retired First Sergeant from my unit's Vietnam days told me about their chaplain. He said the chaplain was still alive and lived in Texas. He was a good chaplain, he said. The chaplain would "accidently" miss the helicopter when he visited them at a distant patrol base and spend the night in the jungle with the troops. They respected him for this. I tucked this detail away and practiced my own version of his technique in Iraq. The next thing he told me surprised me. This old First Sergeant looked me up and down and said, "When he came back from Vietnam, he got divorced." I did not know what to make of that at the time. I just nodded and said I was sorry to hear that. Apparently, news of chaplains' divorces sticks in old soldiers' memories.

There may even be an ancient connection between divorce and military service. A Jewish friend told me her rabbi once told her that David and Bathsheba's adultery is often used to talk about the ethics of adultery and divorce. Apparently, it is believed ancient warriors of the time would give their wives a "Get" a divorce, before going into battle. This would allow Bathsheba the freedom to contract a new marriage while her husband, Uriah, was fighting. I do not think Uriah would have gone along with this line of reasoning, however.

So there I was, a divorced chaplain, begging to do a 36-hour shift at Walter Reed so I could beat the Friday rush-hour(s) traffic out of DC to see my boys in Pennsylvania. I gradually grew used to this club of the divorced. Thus it is with all the clubs we join involuntarily. Slowly, over time, we grow familiar with our surroundings and the people who surround us.

Many of the people I found myself connecting with were, like me, divorced or in some other club. Soldier after soldier connected with me about his or her own heartache, as either the adulterer, the aggrieved spouse, or something in between. For the first time in my life I had a ministry of listening to people who were broken by their relationships breaking before they did.

Soon, we formed a small community there in DC of seekers, or maybe survivors. We were mostly divorced or single. We lived near each other and most of us worked together. One was a Muslim, one a Protestant, one a Catholic, one an agnostic, etc. Our religious affiliations mattered little. What mattered was our experience of war and broken relationships.

As I forged these friendships, I also tried to re-create the community I lost in my divorce. I did this by trying to reconstruct my old family. I tried this several times with different women, trying to shoehorn them into the place my ex-wife held in the family. It took about a year for me to realize the ridiculousness and impossibility of this. I would meet someone, introduce her to my boys, go on a trip with all of us, then miss my pre-divorce family terribly. Then I would break up with my girlfriend. As these women came and went, I found that my friends, this rag-tag bunch of singles and divorced people, stayed true. I began to trust them. They were going through the same changes and chances of life I was going through, after all. Our experience with the army kept us together, that is, until we all started to get our next assignments to different duty stations around the world.

As I reflect on these friendships, I think of how they were the new being for me. They were my spiritual community during a very tumultuous time. They showed me a new vision for human relationships that were loving and open, the kind of relationship that Jesus could have with me.

The Philadelphia Folk Fest has been going strong since 1948. In the farmland of Eastern Pennsylvania, just outside of Philadelphia, thousands of people camp and frolic in the late summer heat for three to five days, taking in the great music and atmosphere. Even though I had grown up a few miles from the fest, I never attended.

The first year I bought a day pass. The second year I camped out. My boys, an army friend, and I pitched two tents and entered into the joy of the fest. I learned how to hula-hoop that week, a strange body movement for a former Marine who grew up in a religion that forbade dancing. I drank through the days and played my guitar at night with the other campers. I only knew a few chords, but that seemed to be enough. My friend jammed on his ukulele, and two neighboring women came over to our campsite and sang along. For me, after fundamentalism, Iraq, and divorce, it was heaven.

Everyone I met loved to dance and be free. They loved spirituality, and many of them told me about their visions and dreams. They were concerned about peace, and looked at me with a kind eye if I told them I had spent some time in Iraq. They loved music, above all, a language that has always transcended creeds and belief systems, time and space. The main thing I miss about fundamentalism is some of the stirring hymns.

That week I saw a very different vision of human relationships. I had fun. I danced crazy-like in the Reggae tent. I hula-hooped for hours. I played with my boys around the campsite. It was, and always will be, a vision of the new being. When I read those words in Tillich, I knew exactly what he was talking about.

The carefree, hippie culture of the folk fest could not have been more different from the military culture I first entered as a teenager. Now I can see both are extremes, and I prefer not to join either exclusively. I am thankful to be out of the active-duty army as much as I am thankful not to be living on a communal compound in the hills of West Virginia. The community I needed was somewhere in between, but these two communities, thankfully, formed very bright buoys for me to steer my ship between.

In Marine Corps marksmanship training, they always said to make bold sight adjustments. That is, when you're trying to zero in on a target with a rifle, it's better to adjust your sights several clicks to the left or right, up or down, than just one click. This way, you can see where the bullet is hitting more clearly, and then adjust accordingly. In order to help me see what I was missing, I needed the straight, unfiltered hippie experience to show me how far into the military I had drifted. Once I made this bold adjustment, I was able to see where I needed to go more clearly. I still have my hula-hoop hooked on my fence outside my Austin apartment. It has even been known to make an appearance in the park and at local music festivals from time to time.

Soon after the folk fest I began to attend Christ Episcopal Church in DC more frequently. This was possible for me because the rector at the parish served across the street from me in Iraq as a chaplain. My connection to him led me to the parish, where I gradually learned to trust some of the members there. One day I realized I could trust the Church.

When I traveled to visit my boys in Pennsylvania, I tried to attend Episcopal churches. Of course, I loved the liturgy and historic connections, but I mostly attended because it was a place I could confess my sins and make a connection with Jesus through his body and blood. The liturgy gave me a sense of safety and continuity I could not find anywhere else in the world at that time.

The seed to return to the Church and begin to trust her members started on a particularly depressing and lonely vacation about a year after my divorce. On a Sunday I stumbled into a historic Episcopal church in northeast Maryland, not far from the campground my boys and I were staying at. Following the service, at the church picnic, a woman came over to me and we began to small talk about where I was from and how I ended up at the church that day. After some chit chat, she said, out of the blue, "You know, someone told me once that when you have some anger, the best thing to do is put it in a suitcase. Take the suitcase up in an airplane, and push the suitcase out the door into the ocean." This was strange advice, especially since I made no mention of my anger. Maybe she could see it in me. It was, strangely, what I needed to hear. It was as if the Spirit of the post-traumatic God was speaking through her. I did not know I was angry until that moment.

In Episcopal churches there is almost always an opportunity to receive Holy Communion, often called the Sacrament. In the ancient Roman army, the *Sacramentum* was the name given the enlistment oath. It was a promise to be faithful in times of great stress and fear. Today's sacraments mean the same thing. They are God's pledge to be faithful to us in times of stress and fear. It was this connection to Jesus that kept me coming back. In those moments at the communion rail or at the coffee hour, I knew I was loved. I knew that whatever I had done wrong, no matter how many times I had failed, God still loved me. I would not have fully known this without the Sacrament of the Church. I would not have fully known this without my experience with the new being, the one place where I could feel my shattered life grasped by the post-traumatic God.

God as the Ground of Being

*Yet in an age of profound, perplexing, and even frightening
change, millions of people are rediscovering from the deepest
human wisdom a simple spiritual reality; we're grounded.*
                    —Diana Butler Bass in *Grounded*

The most critical area of disconnection veterans experience is a shattered relationship with God. As a chaplain, I was expected to have a direct line or, at least, a deep connection with God. I cannot count the times soldiers shushed each other's profanity when I came into the room. It was as if God was listening in those moments. They would ask me to cast out demons, they would call me to pray with their sick children, and they expected me to be there if someone died. The old motto of the Army Chaplain Corps is, "Bringing Soldiers to God and God to Soldiers." I had a ministry of presence, God's grace was expected to happen when I showed up. Once, in Iraq, a young soldier urged me to climb up into his big truck before a combat mission. I climbed up and he showed me the odometer. There, on the odometer plain as day, were the numbers 666. He asked me to do something so I told him to drive it around the block before the mission.

When the link with God is severed in war, chaplains often fake this connection. This can lead to a loss of self-integrity and despair. Paul Tillich's idea of God as the ground of being helped me reconnect with God after I experienced estrangement from God after Iraq.

Luther described his own estrangement from God as *deus absconditus*— the hidden God. But what if God is not only hidden by war, but shattered? Roger Benimoff felt this when he questioned God's compassion. Few chaplains will ever admit a flight to atheism or agnosticism, but most will admit to feelings of estrangement. Some might even admit their image of God was shattered like mine was.

The God Tillich marched to war with was an idol that shattered in the world he described as one of Iron, Fire, and Blood. The God that emerged after God disappeared he called the ground of being. In volume one of his *Systematic Theology,* Tillich walks the reader through a precise philosophical argument exploring how philosophers and theologians explained the ontology of the world and the ontology of humans. From this metaphysical foundation, Tillich moves to explore the meaning of God. He recognizes that whatever becomes a human being's ultimate concern, becomes God. This does not mean God is whatever a person is ultimately concerned about. No, humans often fix their ultimate concern on that which is not ultimate. When this happens, an idol is created. Tillich observed this most often when humans set their ultimate concern on their nation or political party. A nation or a political party becomes demonic and destroys human freedom when it is elevated to god-like status.

Tillich made it clear that the truth about humans cannot be the truth about God. Humans are finite and God is not. God is not a creature like we are creatures. In fact, Tillich argues that God is not a being among other beings. God is the ground of being itself. God, therefore, can be described as the "creative ground" of being. Tillich pointed to the God beyond God that Moses spoke with when God allowed Moses to see him walking by. Moses sees God through the symbols and metaphors God gives us so we can encounter God. Moses cannot see the ground of being itself, or he must die. What he can see is God walking, from behind. For Tillich, the symbol and the deep eternal truth come together in this story.

When Tillich said God is not a being among other beings, but the ground of being itself, he became, according to his disciple Rollo May, "a dangerous man." The substance of the criticism against him was that he was an atheist. After all, he did say, "God does not exist. He is being itself beyond essence and existence. Therefore to argue that God exists is to deny him." Tillich's insistence on this point came from an encounter with the tyrants of the modern age, no doubt a reference to Hitler, who used terror to "transform everything into a mere object, a thing among things, a cog in the machine they control." God is not a tyrant who is trying to transform humans into cogs in God's machine. Rather, God is where a person finds her being, and where a person finds the courage to be oneself.

The major objection to Tillich's conception of God comes from theologians who object to describing God as the ground of being since it too easily falls into pantheism. This pantheistic God is not personal and is nothing like the God in the Bible I described earlier. Tillich acknowledges that the dominant emphasis of the Bible is that God is a living God. These anthropomorphisms are expressions of God's character and must be understood as symbols of the depth and power of God's being itself. Tillich pointed out that the Old Testament prophets spoke of God anthropomorphically while they simultaneously maintained the mystery of the divine ground.

Tillich approached this accusation of pantheism in volume one of his *Systematic Theology*. He said, "Pantheist has become a 'heresy label' of the worst kind." He defined pantheism as seeing God in the creative power of nature, rather than seeing God in everything. God is the absolute substance that is present in everything—the essence of all things. It is meaningless to assert that God is the totality of all things. Tillich disavowed this view because God is then bound into a system of forms and therefore limited. That Tillich's defense against the charge of pantheism convinced his critics is unlikely. Critics have a way of not being swayed. It usually takes an event, often tragic, to shift our thinking in a different direction.

In spite of the criticism in Tillich's day, his views of God as the ground of being have slowly gained traction in American theology. Last year, Diana Butler Bass's *Grounded: Finding God in the World—A Spiritual Revolution* hit the bookshelves to great fanfare. In this beautifully written book, she describes how a purely heavenly God, up there, is inadequate for the needs of today's world. Instead of looking up to find God, we need to look down. In the ground we find a grounded God that is intimately involved in every aspect of our planet's life. On page 17 she introduces her readers to a young World War I army chaplain, Paul Tillich. She describes how he spent more time digging graves than distributing the sacraments. She tells how he said, "A certain God had died on the battle-fields of Europe." Tillich's description just might be finally taking hold of our theological imaginations. I wish I had read this book by Bass during my difficult days of trying to read Tillich with my post-traumatic mind, trying to find God in the broken relationships and self-destruction of my life. According to Bass, God was there all along, in the HESCO bastion and under the canvas floor of my tent at the folk fest.

Even while Tillich argued for seeing God as the ground of being, he also made it clear that no one can develop a doctrine of God from any ontological system. Revelation is required and that is exactly what is given to us in Scripture. If Scripture calls God a person with a name, we must understand that God is a person in "absolute and unconditional partici-pation in everything." Even if we say God is a personal God, we should not understand this to mean God is a person. Tillich noted that the word *persona* was not used in classical theology for God, but for the Trinity. The nineteenth-century concept of a personal God led to the protest of athe-ism. This is why Tillich spoke of a personal God as a confusing symbol.

Veterans who experience a shattered relationship with God may be able to find theological healing through a new understanding of a grounded, post-traumatic God. Tillich's view of God as the ground of being may offer a starting point on such a journey. If Bass's insight is correct, there will be a rise in Christian people finding God in the soil of gardens, and I am sure veterans will be part of this spiritual revolution.

Often, when I meet a veteran for the first time, he or she will say to me, "I'm not religious or anything." Sometimes one will say, "I don't believe all that stuff." There is something about a chaplain's uniform or a clergy collar that sometimes prompts people to state their theological positions in the opening salvos of a conversation. When someone throws down like this, I usually follow Tillich's dictum, ". . . love listens. It is its first task to listen." A fine army chaplain, Robert Leathers, once said, "Listening and love are so close, most people don't know the difference."

When I listen to these warriors tell me what they are not, I often hear some amazing theological themes. Some will say they discovered a love of gardening, or hiking, or some other outdoor activity after they came back from the war. Some of us run marathons or ultra-marathons. Some do Tough Mudder Mud Runs, Spartan races, and ruck marches like the Go-Ruck Challenge. Forest Gump was not the only veteran who ran long distances after war. As they describe these newfound activities, they will often move into theological reflection on the nature of God and ultimate reality. Sometimes their theology, literally their God-talk, will be the opposite of their initial declaration that they are unbelievers. In fact, they are such profound believers that the watered-down religion they grew up with must be rejected at all costs. They have borne witness to the posttraumatic God, but they lack the theological language to describe that God. In time, with this book and others by better theologians than myself, I hope they can.

Post-Traumatic Witness

Scars have the strange power to remind us that our past is real.
—Cormac McCarthy in *All the Pretty Horses*

When I saw those planes crash into the building, it was surreal." Witnesses to 9/11 often use the word "surreal" to describe how they felt on that horrible day. It is as if their minds could not comprehend what was happening in the real world, in reality. This is a normal response to horrific images and events.

During my years as a chaplain on the amputee and psych wards at Walter Reed, I heard many such stories of surreal horror. Being blown up was "weird," "strange," or "just like in the video games." The aftermath was not, however. There was real pain and death. My own experiences in Iraq are often shrouded in fog. I try to remember details with little success. Other details, like the sound of a whirring air conditioner during a rocket attack, are stamped in my memory forever. Our memories are tricky things.

The death of Jesus was a horrific, traumatic event to watch. John is said to have been present for the whole thing. Luke tells us "all his acquaintances" stood at a distance watching. The trauma of Good Friday continues to traumatize the Church. At every Good Friday service I have preached at or attended, I can feel the tightness of breath in the congregation. I can see the constricted faces and the winces when his pain is mentioned. We live Good Friday with Jesus, as best we can. It is wise that we have compartmentalized Good Friday to one day per year. Perhaps it is the only way we can bear it.

John, as the closest observer, tells us about the soldier who pierced Jesus's side with a spear. "Pierced" is a strange word to use in this case. Anyone who uses it has probably not undergone military training with a spear or the modern equivalent, the bayonet. During his first week in the Roman army, the soldier who stuck his spear into Jesus would have practiced the move. I practiced it in Marine Corps Boot Camp in 1994. It has not changed in thousands of years. Feet shoulder width apart, with one foot out front for stability. The thrust must be quick if it is to penetrate skin and bone. It is even more difficult when you are thrusting up, up at a man on a cross. To see one's friend stabbed this way is unthinkable. It would be surreal, at best. The mind would recoil, shrink, divert to something stranger than that. What would you see? What would I see?

John saw blood and water come pouring out of the wound. For two thousand years Christians have pondered the meaning of this flow. The author inserts, right after the piercing in John 19:35, that "He who saw this has testified so that you also may believe." He goes one step further to say, "His testimony is true, and he knows that he tells the truth." Was anyone questioning this? John does not interpret the blood and the water here in his Gospel. Is he pointing this out so the prophecy in the Old Testament— "They will look on the one whom they had pierced?"—will be fulfilled? Later in another book, the same purported author vigorously points to the blood and the water that flowed from Jesus's side as proof of Jesus's veracity. The blood and water, in I John, are witnesses to Jesus's work of redemption. Again, we read the author's protest that he is telling the truth about the event. Does he protest too much? Does he remind us he is telling the truth because so many questioned whether he saw this or not? It is impossible to know. What we can know is that memory of blood and water coming out of Jesus's side is part of John's post-traumatic reflection on the death of his friend and teacher. He alone records it, insisting to everyone he really saw it and you can trust his testimony.

Post-traumatic reflection is often like this. It is selective. Certain details stand out. John did not have access to the word "surreal," but he might have used it if he had. What I see, from my post-traumatic perspective, is a trauma response. Embedded in the text of our holy book is this reaction to trauma. Do traumatized people have something to tell us about the meaning of the crucifixion? This one, John, certainly thought so.

The theological reflection on John's post-traumatic memory is still happening today. What does the blood and water mean? What does it symbolize, medically or metaphorically? The classic hymn "Rock of Ages" offers this reflection:

> Rock of Ages, cleft for me,
> Let me hide myself in Thee;
> Let the water and the blood,
> From Thy riven side which flowed,
> Be of sin the double cure,
> Save me from its guilt and power.

The early Church reflected often on the trauma of Christ. The suffering they experienced must have been the subtext of every such reflection. All their beliefs about who Jesus was came out of their reflection on these stories.

By the time I John is written, this blood and water trauma story informs the early Christian teaching about Jesus's divinity. Later, some verses are allegedly added to the blood and water description in I John to shore up the Trinitarian argument with this story. The post-traumatic reflection of the early Church resulted in the theology we confess in the creeds every Sunday.

Post-Traumatic Resurrection

The wound is the place where the Light enters you.

—Rumi

John's account of the post-Easter Jesus are as surreal as his account of the crucifixion. The stories of Jesus preserved by the Johannine community were, from the beginning, the account of a traumatized person. John tells us in Chapter 20 that the disciples locked themselves inside the house for fear of the Jews. They were in fear for their lives since they were the next likely victims of crucifixion. Since Jesus was childless, there were only disciples to mop up after killing the King of the Jews. Thinking you are going to be crucified and being crucified are equally traumatizing. The anxiety of impending doom is crippling and is the hallmark symptom of PTSD.

I remember this feeling in Iraq, shortly after I arrived. A few months before I arrived, an Army dental officer, a dentist, had been killed. I knew that even though I was a chaplain, and God was on my side, I would not get any special treatment from the enemy. An article in the newspaper came out while I was there saying intel (military intelligence) reports indicated the enemy was targeting chaplains. Walking around Baghdad without a rifle was a pretty clear sign I was a chaplain, not to mention the crosses on my helmet and chest. I was rarely afraid of dying over there; I was afraid of not doing my job when all hell broke loose. Did I have what it takes to save lives, to rescue the wounded, to be calm under pressure when the deal went down? The slow drip of anxiety in the back of my brain affected everything I did over there. It still affects me when I assume everything is about to fall apart and my whole world is tottering on the brink of destruction. This feeling was useful over there, not so much here. Sometimes I am self-destructive. Sometimes I try to engineer situations where other people have to fail me. I self-sabotage my success so I will get what I see: doom and failure.

The Rt. Rev. Andy Doyle, Bishop of Texas, writes about Schrodinger's Church in his *A Generous Community: Being the Church in a New Missionary Age.* Schrodinger's Church is simply an extension of his cat that is both alive and dead at the same time. Doyle wisely pronounces that we will get the Church we see. This is true of everything in life, whether a cat in a box or a church. We are more likely to see what we believe than believe what we see. As St. Augustine said, "Understanding is the reward of faith. Therefore, seek not to understand that you may believe, but believe that you may understand."

The disciples are restless, anxious, and fearful. Seeing what happened to Jesus, whether close up or farther away, did something to them. It is in this post-traumatic context that Jesus says, "Peace be with you."

On Sundays, when the Church gathers, we pass the peace. These are the first words new priests say to their congregations. I said these words when I was ordained at Christ Episcopal Church in Georgetown, DC. I said these words this past Sunday to dozens of people, accompanied by hugs and handshakes. Jesus says these words to his tiny group of trauma-tized disciples. Jesus knows what we need to hear.

About a year after Iraq, right before my divorce was finalized, I was in deep despair. I had been writing God with a lower case "g" for sev-eral months. I was trying to find a way to solve the problem of divorce. I was terrified of being divorced, the unforgivable sin in the fundamentalist community of my youth. About once a week, I went to the top of the army hospital to have a conversation with a woman who worked in the personnel office. I told her about my impending divorce while updating some personal information on my Identification Card, and we began to talk about life and relationships, mine particularly. I shared how nervous I was about dating or remarriage since this one had been such a disaster in the end. Because my wife left me for another man, I assumed I was a less than adequate lover—why else would she leave me? I remember the woman laughing and telling me, "Honey, your wife didn't leave you because of that." She repeated it until I grasped what she was saying. Her words of peace stick with me to this day. We need to speak words of peace to people who are traumatized. Our words always have more power than we know.

The next thing Jesus does is show them his hands and his side. John does not say he showed them his wounds. That happens later, when Jesus encounters Thomas. The Greek word for Jesus's wounds in the gospels is not *trauma,* but one of several Greek words for wounds. The Greek word, *trauma,* is used only by Luke to describe the wounds of the man left for dead by the robbers in the parable of the Good Samaritan. In this brutal attack by robbers, *trauma* is a fitting word for the wounds the traveler received from those who "left him for dead." Since the ancient world was a violent one, it is not surprising there are so many different words for "wound."

Before the crucifixion, John tells us Mary anointed Jesus with perfume. The Greek text in John says it was myrrh. The Christmas carol "We Three Kings" says, "Myrrh is mine, its bitter perfume/breathes a light of gathering gloom." The gloomy scent filled the room as she anointed ("rubbed" in the Greek) the ointment on his feet, drying it with her hair. The myrrh was made by cutting the scrubby plant with a knife. The knife must cut down to the second layer of its flesh. From this wound, sap begins to seep. The sap dries and is then collected several weeks later. The very process used to make myrrh speaks to the sacrificial nature of Mary's gift. She knows the trauma that awaits. She knows she is doing this for his burial.

When Jesus appears in the Upper Room after his resurrection, our storyteller, John, relates how they all rejoiced. Luke's version says they were "startled and terrified" when Jesus appeared and said, "Peace be with you." Luke also says they thought him to be a ghost. Unlike John, the author of Luke never claims to be a witness to this event. After watching Jesus's crucifixion, it is little wonder they were terrified at his reappearance. What could they trust anymore, if not the certainty of death? Shock and terror seem to be the predominant responses to the risen Jesus. While I am sure there are many reasons for this, could one of them be that traumatized people do not like to be reminded of the traumatic event in any way, shape, or form?

There are times when I run by a dump truck and smell its diesel fuel and hear the rumble and rattle of its engine. Immediately, I am back in Baghdad about to roll outside the wire. I am no longer startled by loud noises, but I tear up, then sob, whenever I watch fireworks. Traumatized people shrink the world down to a safe size. The problem with this is that the world becomes very small. With more and more triggers, there are more and more things to avoid. There are disconnections and shattered narratives. Stories jump around, paying little mind to the structure of a timeline. When I read the post-Easter narratives, this is what I see. The Gospels are more like the writing of Vietnam veteran and writer Tim O'Brien than what we might expect from even a pre-modern historian. What else should we expect from a post-traumatic community?

The witness of the post-traumatic gospels points again and again to the wounds of Jesus. The wounded Jesus understands the wounds we receive in war. The wounded Jesus demonstrates what God does with wounded people—he raises them from the dead. God is the God of second, third, and fourth chances. Jesus stretched out his arms on the hard wood of the cross so that all may come into his saving embrace.

If we are sure Jesus had, and still has, visible wounds, should we not be open to the idea that he has invisible wounds too? He was betrayed by his friend and disciple, Judas. Every Sunday we gather and repeat the words, "On the night he was betrayed, he took bread." Betrayed people never trust anyone again. Betrayed people are hyper-vigilant, expecting it to happen again. Their trust was used against them and they will never let it happen again. Just as Jesus's wounded hands and side were healed in the Resurrection, so his invisible wounds would have been healed too. But this is a difficult concept to grasp. We may assume that the healing of a soul wound would leave no trace, but this is not the case. All wounds leave scars—and a soul wound, like the wounding from a betrayal, leaves a scar. If a soul wound from a betrayal is healed, it means the person can trust again. Even though healing has happened, the marks are still there, the pathways of the soul are still cut deep, and the scar tissue bears witness to the wound and the strength that now exists to replace the bleeding wound.

The word "excruciating" is linked linguistically to crucifixion. Jesus was crucified, which means he was not executed, he was tortured to death. Execution is quick, a hangman's noose or an axe to an outstretched neck. No, crucifixion is a slow process that warps and twists the mind. All the sadistic torturers of the world could not have devised a worse experience for a human. Crucifixion was a demise fit only for slaves and enemies of the state. Roman citizens were immune from the cruel grasp of the cross. What did his mind do to escape the pain? How did his body contort itself to absorb the sharp ache of his suffering? All physical torture is psychological torture too. The war on terror has offered Americans a chance to discuss whether torture is beneficial, ethical, wrong or right. As a nation we are divided on this question. Why is that, when we consider that our Lord was tortured by soldiers who were just doing their job? We know very little from the evangelist about the torture of the cross. They do not drag out the descriptions of his physical suffering. They simply say he was crucified. For anyone who had seen a real one, that was enough.

While the specifics of cross height, hand placement, and other gruesome details are missing, we have four accounts of Jesus's final words from the cross. They are short, spoken by someone who had very little lung capacity. They haunt us still, inspiring us to reflect on his sacrifice and love.

While I can make a connection between my own invisible wounds and the invisible wounds of Christ, I can hardly compare them. It even feels silly to type these words, with any hint that my experience of life was anything like his. However, each of us, each veteran, each person, must be willing to own their story. Of course I was not on Omaha Beach on D-Day. That still does not mean I am not worthy to have struggles and difficulties from my war. I was never tortured, physically or mentally. Obviously, I was never crucified either. I was, however, betrayed. I was helpless, many times, to protect myself and the lives of those around me.

Not only did I experience this helplessness, I also inflicted pain on others. Army veteran Daniel Crimmins puts it bluntly, "You grow up wanting to be Luke Skywalker, then realize you've become a stormtrooper for the Empire." My presence in the war legitimized the killing we did. I was not on the tip of the spear by any means, only a few are, but I was pushing the spear from further back on the shaft. We all were. An entire nation goes to war, not just the warriors. Although we set them apart for their sacred priesthood of blood, we are all in it together. We all need reconciliation after war—all of us.

Jesus came to me with his wounds and it showed me my wounds could become the source of healing for others. Touching his wounds is uncomfortable, but we cannot know Jesus any other way. There is not an unwounded Jesus. The one who comes to us with open hands does so in order for us to see his wounds, in order to embrace us.

Post-Traumatic Pentecost

No one ever told me that grief felt so like fear.
—C. S. Lewis in A Grief Observed

The highlight of the account of Pentecost in the Acts of the Apostles is Peter's sermon. Peter is transformed in this story from an inept, bungling disciple into a powerful apostle. Peter himself credits this transformation to the Holy Spirit that animates him. His sermon is pointed directly at the people who crucified Jesus. At the end he gives them a chance to repent and be baptized. His words have their desired effect and thousands are baptized.

We remember Peter in the Garden of Gethsemane, attacking the High Priest's servant Malchus with a sword. Only John tells us it was Peter. Was it embarrassment that kept the other evangelists silent about the slasher's identity?

When the posse came to arrest Jesus, Peter stepped between his friend and the threat. This is what warriors do. They step between the loved one and those that seek to do them harm. It happens again and again in combat. It is as natural as breathing. But Peter was not a warrior. He missed.

I learned in Marine Corps boot camp how to fight with a knife. That is likely what Peter was carrying. Even if it was a "sword," it is unlikely it had a blade longer than twelve inches. When you attack with a blade, you either slash or stab. From the account in the Gospels, Peter slashed straight down with great force—a strange strike indeed. The servant, Malchus, may have been wearing a breastplate, thus the strike to the head. He must not have been wearing a helmet, a foolish oversight for a soldier going to make an arrest. He must have done something to draw Peter's specific ire. We cannot know more than what is given to us in all four Gospels. Peter was not skilled with a sword and had likely never used one before in a real fight. The shame of his inept defense must have been enormous. As an inadequate defender, he denies he knows Jesus in the courtyard during his trial and scourging. This man who pledged to go with Jesus all the way to death, left him when things got too hot. As Jesus moves toward the place of crucifixion, Peter slinks away into the darkness. This is what moral injury looks like. Moral injuries are those things "done and left undone." In war these things are legion. Not helping a friend in need can haunt us for years and years.

In the depths of his shame, moral injury, and regret, Jesus restores Peter at the Sea of Galilee. Peter emerges from his shame and trauma to be a powerful witness to reconciliation. The reconciliation of Peter is not easy. Jesus's blessing comes first with a great catch of fish. Then Peter puts his clothes on and jumps into the water to meet Jesus on shore. They all gather there and Jesus breaks bread. Then Jesus asks Peter three questions, mirrors of his three denials. The words of reconciliation are as painful as the words of denial. Peter is restored and is commissioned as an apostle to follow Jesus even unto the cross.

Judas, who also betrays Jesus, hangs himself. If he had only waited. Suicide and shame go together. Surviving a traumatic event usually means that other people were killed in it. Survivor guilt eats at the soul and plunges veterans into a deeper spiral of hopelessness and worthlessness. Suicide is not unexpected and continues to plague the veteran community.

My own struggles with suicide happened after Iraq. On several occasions a perfect storm of crises have engulfed me and suicide seemed, at the moment, to be the only way out. It was like I was in a tunnel. On one such occasion, I was aware of how deep in the tunnel I was. I knew that I "shouldn't" kill myself, because it would hurt my children, but a part of my mind was obsessed with the idea. Every few days I would contemplate suicide. Sometimes I would plan it. This brought great relief to me and made me feel better. I knew this from suicide-prevention classes I taught in the army, but it was different to experience it firsthand. Thankfully, those suicidal feelings pushed me to seek help and take action on the areas of my life that felt out of my control.

One of the things I did was quit my job. After leaving active duty in the army and moving to Texas, I had accepted a job at a hospital. At the time I thought it would be a good career move, but I was less sure I wanted to do that particular job. It turned out to be very stressful for me, since I realized, after a few months, that it was not my calling. I thought it was, but it was not. I had discerned my way out, but the thought of not having a paycheck scared me. I did not have another job lined up, so I kept at it, trying to be a success.

While I was struggling at work, another Iraq veteran was struggling with me. I met Eric on the first day of orientation. We bonded as fellow veterans and I checked in on him occasionally at the hospital cafeteria where he worked as a chef. One day he was not there. I called him and he told me he had gotten in a fight with his supervisor and quit. Veterans have a hard time with employment for many reasons. I certainly did. I was good at showing up on time, which is fifteen minutes early, but I couldn't handle criticism from my supervisors. My fragility reminds me of Peter, when he denied he knew Jesus. In the military I quickly learned who I could trust and who I couldn't. When I left the army, I did not trust anyone. I assumed the worst about people, and since we were never in a life or death situation, I could never figure out if they were worthy of my trust.

When Jesus restores Peter after his resurrection, Peter is empowered. His shame disappears and he boldly preaches to a tough crowd. The Church today needs to proclaim this same message of reconciliation to veterans. Most veterans carry something shameful from their military service. The chaos of combat and the monotony of deployments are fertile ground for unexpected failures and letdowns. The YouTube videos of these events come back to us in the night.

I first heard of Brené Brown a few years after I came home from Iraq. Her work on shame, a concept I refer to frequently in this book, named what I was feeling. Before I read her work, I would have called that feeling anger, or anxiety. Brown says shame is the intensely painful feeling that we are unworthy of love and belonging. It disconnects us from others, and self-destruction is not far behind. Shame might be the most primitive human emotion we all feel—and the one no one wants to talk about. But Peter talks about it.

When Peter preaches his bold sermon at Pentecost, he mentions God's actions in the crucifixion and resurrection. In Acts 2:22–24, he says that God did miracles through Jesus and that Jesus was "handed over to you according to the definite plan and foreknowledge of God." Then he says, "But God raised him up." Peter's understanding of how God was involved in the crucifixion is fascinating to me. He says that the crucifixion was due to the definite plan and foreknowledge of God. Perhaps he is reflecting on all the statements he heard from Jesus about his death as he marched to Jerusalem. Perhaps he was thinking about how Jesus's death fulfilled the prophet's predictions. Or perhaps he was doing what I saw many solders doing in Iraq.

Over and over again, I would gently query the soldiers in my battalion about how safe they felt when they faced the dangers of that place. When the subject of danger came up, they would invariably invoke the mantra of the warrior, "When it's your time, it's your time." This fatalistic response to the uncertainties of combat was a source of consolation. By stating that the timing of one's death was in God's foreknowledge, even in God's plans, brought peace. Otherwise, the anxiety of the uncertain situation would be unbearable. By stating this they were not saying they were not going to take all the precautions necessary for survival. They were simply stating the one thought that put their mind at ease. By placing the responsibility in God's hands, they could focus on the more pressing concerns of their mission.

Perhaps Peter is doing this same thing, as crucifixion is still a very strong possibility for him and his fellow disciples. He is, after all, preaching about the crucifixion in the very city in which it happened. Perhaps his sermon will be interrupted by the same soldiers who crucified Jesus? This post-traumatic sovereignty helped him in the moment as it has helped many other Christians since. The doctrine of God's sovereign control in the universe seems to rise in popularity in the face of persecution and hardship. When we are at ease and in comfort, we are less inclined to need God to have such a close hold on world events. Undoubtedly, this works differently for every person. For Peter, it seems to be working well, healing and soothing his damaged heart and mind.

His sermon in Acts drives home one major point, "It's all your fault!" He builds his case that Jesus is the promised one, the Messiah of Israel. Then he points at them and accuses them of crucifying him. They repent en masse, "cut to the heart" by his powerful point. Peter blames his listeners for the death of his friend and teacher. This always strikes me as strange. It is unlikely the Roman soldiers from the crucifixion detail are in the crowd. It is unlikely the Sanhedrin, Pilate, Herod, or Caiaphas are in the crowd either. The people in the crowd did not crucify Jesus, so why would Peter tell them they did? Why would they agree with him and repent?

Peter, the post-traumatic preacher, sounds a lot like many of the soldiers I listened to after their trauma. After an IED killed a friend, I would hear a stream of blame on all the Iraqis. Grief after trauma casts a wide net of blame. The grieving place blame on the enemy, the Iraqis, the war, the army, just about everyone, hoping to find someone to pay back. Sometimes, this grief spills over into war atrocities where warriors attempt to exact revenge on the village where their friend died. The more personal the loss, the wider the net of blame is cast.

Peter includes everyone in the responsibility for Jesus's death. He includes himself. The beauty of his post-traumatic sermon, however, is that he seeks their repentance and reconciliation, not retribution. He does not call for the crowd to be crucified but to become followers of Jesus the Christ. People on the other side of trauma can be very bold. Post-traumatic people often have the power to speak loudly about the love and forgiveness they have found. It is time that the veterans of these recent wars rise up and proclaim the love of God to the world. It is time we become agents and heralds of reconciliation between races, creeds, sexual preferences, and our enemies. We have the post-traumatic power to do this.

Post-Traumatic Leaders

All of these lines across my face/tell you the story of who I am.
—Brandie Carlisle, "The Story"

Every Sunday I look out at the congregation from the safety of my clergy bench. The people of God have gathered to worship. They have left houses and apartments to come here. Some have even left sidewalks and park benches. A few of them have left war zones, foreign or domestic. Some have a spouse that beat them this past week. Some have been threatened, cheated on, lied to. Some have watched a loved one, a child, a husband, a partner, or a wife, suffer with alcohol abuse. Every one of them has a story. I only know a small percentage of them. What stories are behind those intent, staring, praying, hard-to-read faces? Who can know them all?

Church leaders are expected to know some, if not all, of them. We are often the first person people turn to in trauma and crisis. In my experience, people tell us their stories when they trust us. The slightest hint that we will disclose a story keeps most traumatized people silent. They smile, they nod, they shake our hand, but they never let us in.

In my work with veterans, both inside the Army and outside it, I have found deep listening to be my only tool. Listening is not easy, especially when we have stories of our own. The two years I spent in clinical pastoral education drilled this into me. I am not a natural listener. I like to process verbally, much to the annoyance of the introverts in my life, who process internally.

Listening is difficult because we have stories too. Our traumas, our losses, our stories lie just beneath the surface of our small talk. We hear a story, we share a story—that is how friends talk. But the post-traumatic leader must lead with listening. Our stories must be set aside to privilege the story of the person to whom we are listening. This does not mean we do not have friends. This does not mean we do not go to therapy to tell our stories. We need to do this. However, when someone presents their trauma to us, when they open the door of their experiences to us, we must listen.

Post-traumatic ministry is listening, and everyone can do it. I have a very narrow range of traumatic experiences. My experience in war was twelve months. I never went ashore on D-Day. I never jumped on a grenade during the Tet Offensive. I only have my own experience. While I cannot tell a trauma survivor that I understand or that I know what they feel, I can draw on my own experiences of horror and trauma in order to see the person.

It is remarkable how many times in the Gospels Jesus saw people. Jesus saw Simon, Peter, and Andrew and he called them to follow him. Jesus saw Peter's mother-in-law and healed her of her fever. He turned and saw the woman who grabbed the hem of his robe and healed her. He saw a large crowd and had compassion on them. He saw a poor widow putting her two mites in the temple treasury and he blessed her. He saw the city of Jerusalem and wept for her. On the cross, he saw his mother there, and the disciple whom he loved, and he spoke to them. Jesus was always looking, seeing what was in front of him. Every day we meet people with trauma, but we do not see them.

Post-traumatic leaders must be on their own healing pilgrimage. When I started the first Episcopal Veterans Fellowship group at St. David's Episcopal Church in Austin, Texas, I soon realized I needed help. Listening to my fellow veterans' stories of grief, trauma, and loss triggered my own stories and losses. Many were still unresolved. Many still are. Unexpectedly, I plunged into another round of depression and withdrawal. I wondered if I had done the right thing, starting this group. I knew we were helping veterans—that was obvious—but I wasn't sure I would survive it. With the help of a counselor I started to attend group sessions at the Veterans Administration outpatient hospital. These groups, led by a psychologist, helped me process some of my own grief and loss. I try to stay on the healing journey every day, as best as I can. I can look back today with thanks that I survived. I can look back today with thanks because people came to my aid when I needed them most.

Post-traumatic leaders must do their own spiritual work and we can be sure that original content will emerge. This can be seen in the history of the Christian Church. Martin of Tours was a fourth-century Roman soldier, likely a cavalry officer. He was drawn to Christianity at an early age but could not be baptized because he chose to follow his father into the army. Because of his father's career, Martin was named for Mars, the god of war.

This little god of war served nobly, eventually ending up in France. On a cold day he came upon a beggar who was naked. Martin responded to this person's need by cutting his cape in half with his sword. He gave half of it (the lower half, I presume) to the beggar and rode back to the barracks dressed only in his half. My veteran readers can imagine what his fellow cavalry soldiers said about his little cape when he came through the door.

That night he had a dream where Jesus extended the offer of baptism to him. He was baptized soon after and continued in the army for either a short time or a long time. Hagiography, the history of the saints, being what is, is unclear on this point. If he stayed in too long, it would have made early hagiographers nervous, since true Christians were expected to leave the army instantly after baptism. It is likely he stayed in for many years, thus creating a conundrum for his community. He finally left after refusing to fight in a battle. He was imprisoned and chastised for not being willing to fight. Instead of fighting, he offered to stand between the armies unarmed. This led to his discharge from the service. He became a monk and eventually a bishop.

His influence in the Church and world remains. His half-cape became a relic and was the origin of the words "chapel" and "chaplain." We know it was blue since the blue in the French flag is from St. Martin's cape. The treaty ending World War I was signed on St. Martin's Day, November 11. Eventually Armistice Day became Veterans Day in the United States, making Martin the patron saint of veterans.

In March 2016 eight veterans gathered in Brenham, Texas, at an old Franciscan monastery to take vows in the Hospitallers of St. Martin, a Christian community for ministry to veterans. Lynn Smith-Henry, an army veteran, and I prayed about forming this community three years before, so it was exciting to see it born in Brenham. The Rt. Rev. James Magness, bishop of the Armed Forces and Federal Chaplaincies, was there to bless the eight novices as they entered the novitiate of the community. It is our hope that these new monastics will form the leadership corps for veterans' ministry in the Episcopal Church. Like Martin of old, we do not know where God is leading us. We only know that there are veterans who need reconciliation and love. We want to be part of this mission.

Another example of a post-traumatic leader is St. Francis. Francis was not always a saint. He was, in fact, a rich kid. He was born in 1182 to a father who was a successful silk merchant. His father set his son up for success. As was the custom of the day, he suited up in his armor and went to battle against a neighboring city-state in Italy. His side lost, and he was taken as a prisoner of war (POW). He spent a year in a dungeon, unsure of whether he would live or die. One only needs to read the memoir of a POW, such as David Carey, one of my former parishioners, to know the psychological, spiritual, and physical strain of captivity.

Carey's memoir, *The Way We Choose: Lessons for Life from a POW's Experience,* chronicles his imprisonment in the Hanoi Hilton for over five years. Carey says, "We were not treated in accordance with any agreements on the treatment of prisoners of war. . . . We were interrogated on occasion, beaten on rare occasions, and tortured on very rare occasions." During the intense tortures of his early days in captivity he recalls, "I begged them to kill me. But they wouldn't kill me. They just hurt me."

We don't know what Francis endured in that medieval prison. Was this the start of his spiritual journey? If the testimony of every POW can be trusted, it was. The loss of one's strength can do wonders for the spirit. The deprivations of the body can lead to strength of the soul. Francis had the power to take life, to kill, on the battlefield. In the dungeon he depended on the goodwill of his jailors for his very breath. Who can know what this is like?

I once had a patient who served in World War II and spent two years as a POW in Germany. He told me they would have a formation every evening where the guards would tell them they would be killed in the morning. He said their speech got to some of the guys. He told me it killed one. "He was so afraid. He believed them." I asked him if he believed it. "No," he said, "I never believed those bastards." The first casualty in war is truth, and in a POW camp truth does not exist. Rumors abound, and the deepest wounds are in the mind.

We do not know what Francis endured. No record of his time there exists. Whatever happened, he emerged, like all who come home from war, to resume the life he left. This lasted for a short time. Then, as they will do, another war began and he proceeded to put his armor on again. It was then that God called him. He embraced this call, renouncing all privilege and comfort. He founded a community devoted to service and the Eucharist. His influence is still felt today—even the Pope wants to be like him.

Ignatius of Loyola was born a year before Columbus landed in the West Indies for the first time. He worked as a hired soldier, a mercenary, fighting the endless war between Spain and France. In 1521, while standing on a castle wall, a small cannon ball struck his leg, shattering it. During his convalescence, he began to read about the life of Christ and the saints. His numerous surgeries—one involving sawing off a protruding bone—and infections made recovery slow. The longer he lay in bed, the more he read. The more he read, the more he devoted his life to Christ.

It was on this bed of near death and recovery that he began to write his *Spiritual Exercises,* a book that empowered the laity to follow Christ in an age of spiritual crisis.

After recovering, he made a pilgrimage Jerusalem, where he left his sword in the shrine of Our Lady, never to look back. His mark on the world was made in the years following his conversion. He formed a community of faithful students, out of which the Jesuits, the Society of Jesus, sprung. The lives he touched, and still touches, are legion. In the economy of God, he was a billionaire.

Like most examples of warriors-turned-saints in history, the men outnumber the women. Most warriors, after all, have been men. This does not mean that women have not been in combat. Almost every battlefield in history has had female participants. These women often played supporting roles, but occasionally served in combat disguised as young men. Women have witnessed the horrors of war since time immemorial. They have rescued the wounded, comforted the dying, buried the dead, and carried supplies. They have been raped by victorious soldiers and seen their sons and husbands borne away in the red tide of war. Women know combat trauma.

Today, women serve in combat. I served with many brave women in Iraq and I am thankful for their protection of me, since I was a chaplain, and their devotion to their military duties. They kept many of us alive with their commitment to the mission and their fellow war fighters.

One notable saint is Florence Nightingale, who arrived as a nurse during the Crimean War. She inherited the sick and dying from three armies. She acutely diagnosed the hospital as unsanitary and worked tirelessly to reduce infection and the spread of diseases. The death rate dropped significantly, and Florence was lauded as a hero. What she saw in that hospital in Crimea is documented in her extensive journals. Over 4,000 soldiers died the first winter after she arrived. The small staff cared for them and buried them all. She stayed with many of them, taking her lamp from bedside to bedside. This was not a pristine scene from a painting, but a noisy, putrid, and disturbing place. Those who clean up the mess of war know the most about war.

While on an all-night shift at Walter Reed, I was alerted a new shipment of wounded warriors was arriving from the hospital in Germany. The severely wounded from Iraq and Afghanistan would be sent to the American army hospital in Landstuhl, Germany. Once stabilized there, they would come to a stateside hospital. Walter Reed received most of the psych and amputee patients. Burn victims usually went to Brook Army Medical Center in San Antonio.

I silenced my beeper and went down to meet the wounded. Walter Reed had an ambulance that was truly a converted tractor-trailer. It was huge. In the back were stacks of bunks, wheelchair space, and seats for the ambulatory patients. Most of the psych patients could walk, but the others usually could not. One of the receiving social workers briefed me about the patients. Several were stable, one was possibly dying. He was only sent to Walter Reed because his family was meeting him there, to be with him if his death was indeed soon. They did not know for sure. No one ever really does.

I said I would stay with him. I sat next to his battered body, peppered with blast wounds. His skin was red from the sheer number of them. His breathing tube breathed for him, his eyes closed in a drug-induced coma. I waited with him while his family made their way to the hospital for their tragic reunion after war.

I did not know what to do. I prayed out loud. Who knows what the patients hear. I always assume they hear more than I assume. In a meditative state I began to sing Taizé songs. Their repetitive cadence, line after line. "Stay with me/remain here with me/watch and pray/watch and pray" kept playing over in my voice. It was as if I no longer sang it, but another, more compassionate chaplain who was in the room with me. I felt something, but not enough compassion for the size of the moment. I trusted the song and the community that wrote it. I trusted the God who called me to be a chaplain. I trusted the breathing tube inserted down the young man's windpipe.

The succession of thousands of these young bodies must have had its effect on Florence Nightingale. The fervor with which she conducted her reforms reflects the urgency born in war. After the war she devoted her life to the sick and dying. She was an early leader in nursing education and wrote extensively about best practices. On the centennial of her death, 2010, the United Nations declared the "International Year of the Nurse." A committed Anglican, she is commemorated on August 12 in the Episcopal Church.

The post-traumatic leader must be a listener, but the post-traumatic leader must also take action. Florence used to describe herself as a "man of action." The leaders I have mentioned—Martin, Francis, Ignatius, Florence Nightingale—have one thing in common: war and action. They took their experiences, good and bad, and found God leading them to serve the world.

If you do take action, you will face opposition. Everyone who ever did anything on this planet has faced opposition. When you hit the gas, lots of folks will hit the brakes. When I arrived in Texas, shortly after leaving active duty in the army chaplaincy, I struggled to find a place to serve. I worked part time, went to school full time, but struggled to find a place. I soon found out that my army experience counted for very little. I suppose prospective civilian employers thought I had been driving a tank around for eight years. What could I do to convince them I had been doing what they did, answering emails, talking to people, attending meetings. Of course, I was doing all this in Iraq and in army facilities, in uniform. The military-civilian gap yawned wide for me. I despaired often of finding a place in the world after war. I tried to go back on active duty. I tried to get deployed. I was unable to make this happen.

That was when I found that the 2009 General Convention of the Episcopal Church resolved that every diocese was encouraged to form an Episcopal Veterans Fellowship. I leaped with joy. Surely, this was something I could do. I went to the bishop, half hoping he would appoint me as the "Veterans Missioner," a position I had outlined in a brief write-up. The bishop was encouraging, insightful, and kind to me. He blessed my efforts to go form this community. He recommended I start the group at St. David's Church in downtown Austin.

My vision was to form a group of women and men on the long journey home from war. This missional community would focus on healing the spiritual wounds of war through Pilgrimages of Reconciliation, trust-filled community groups, and the ancient practice of lament. The ultimate purpose was to form a community that understands its own spiritual journey in war and homecoming. I hoped to foster a renewed connection to Christ and his Church.

Since I was a full-time student at Seminary of the Southwest, working on a Master's of Arts in Religion, I applied for a grant from the Episcopal Evangelism Society, a foundation that helps to fund students involved in outreach. Their generous gift of $5,000 covered our advertising and food-related costs for two years.

Our first meeting was a Pilgrimage of Remembrance and Reconciliation at St. David's. We advertised on the radio and tried to get the word out about our new group, the Episcopal Veterans Fellowship. Eight people came to the first meeting and the group was born. From the beginning the veterans who attended this first meeting have formed the leadership circle of the group.

My original vision was to conduct literal pilgrimages, hikes from St. David's to war memorials in the Austin area. After the first meeting the veterans, especially the Vietnam and World War II veterans, made it very clear that they weren't interested in any physical activity, especially since it was summer in Austin with temperatures in the upper 90s. I was disappointed. After all, it was the pilgrimage model that I envisioned in the long months of preparation. They were, however, interested in meeting together and building community.

We started our meetings off with snacks or a meal, as well as an honest check-in. I quickly found that my vulnerability about my struggles offered an invitation for others to be open about theirs. Referrals to mental-health professionals and other resources were an integral part of the check-in. Next, I facilitated a discussion that addressed the spiritual dimensions of war and homecoming. This was followed by a time of lament, where veterans shared a poem, a song, or another work of art that captured their feelings and experiences. Finally, we prayed the Office of Compline, a short prayer service infused with military themes of protection and safety. This model became the model that has replicated itself to three other parishes that currently have Episcopal Veterans Fellowship groups.

Through this process I learned that I had to listen carefully to discern the needs of the community, no matter what my needs and visions were at the time. I also learned the power of laypersons to start their own groups and carry the ministry into the world. I started the first two groups, with key support from the Rev. Robert Chambers, the son of a Korean War veteran, then a deacon and now a priest, and Episcopal seminarian Lynn Smith-Henry, an army veteran. These two men provided the early community for me. Motivated laypersons, Warren, Steve, and Robert, started the second two groups. Steve leads a group at St. Christopher's in Killeen, Texas, the city that includes the world's largest military base, Ft. Hood. He describes his community as being "like the surface of Mars compared to non-military communities." In this unique environment, Steve and the Rev. Janice Jones, the rector, focus more on providing authentic community for active-duty soldiers, veterans, family members, and spouses. In this highly transient community, they recognized the needs and responded. Clergy support was key to the success of these additional groups. Veterans are used to a hierarchy of command and support, so without the rector's support, it is not possible to form a group of veterans within a parish.

Starting anything new requires patience and a "beginner mind." Success is defined as a community that trusts each other and is doing the spiritual work of reconciliation themselves. The stories of reconciliation are astounding to me. On three occasions veterans told me the group was responsible for saving their lives as they planned their suicide. I learned that warriors aren't afraid of dying, but they are afraid of being alone. A group's effectiveness comes out of its safety. Laughter and tears are my indicators of whether participants feel safe.

During the time I was creating safety for the group, my own safety was difficult to maintain. The intense sharing of combat experiences in the group brought up many of my own memories and the symptoms followed. I soon realized that I had to engage my own issues with war and homecoming if I was to be of any use to the community. I began attending a group at the VA hospital and other counseling appointments. This helped me process my own issues so I could continue leading the community.

If I were to do anything differently, I would have found lay leaders earlier and spent more time with them, preparing them for the ministry. My worries about well-meaning folk hijacking the group were mostly unfounded, but those worries made it difficult for me to share the vision with others. More trust in God, less fear of failure, is a succinct account of what I learned.

One book that helped me was *Missional, Monastic, and Mainline* by Elaine Heath. Another book I picked up recently is *The Wisdom of Stability: Rooting Faith in a Mobile Culture,* by Jonathan Wilson-Hartgrove. Seeing the building of community as the primary goal of a ministry gave me somewhere to focus when I couldn't tell if anything worthwhile was happening. To launch a new group, no amount of advertising or publicity will replace authentic human relationships.

Any book about war and homecoming points to the need for rituals of reconciliation after combat. A recent notable volume in this canon is Robert Meagher's *Killing from the Inside Out: Moral Injury and Just War.* The religious resource we've used is the Sacrament of Reconciliation in the Book of Common Prayer. This sacrament explains why this community is a function of the Church. Biblical accounts of Jesus restoring Peter after he abandons and denies his Lord have helped me understand how reconciliation works in a community of veterans. Seeing the veterans' stories in the stories of Scripture reminds me of the sacredness of our work. The Rev. Christian Hawley, himself a veteran, preached at a Pilgrimage of Remembrance and Reconciliation that veterans coming home from war have an experience similar to Lazarus coming back to life. Veterans share this experience of coming back to a world that cannot relate well to Lazarus's experience. Finding the community story in God's story keeps me motivated for further outreach and service.

While starting the Episcopal Veterans Fellowship, I often repeated a quote from D.L. Moody in my head: "I like the way I do it better than the way you don't do it." My internal gallery of critics, and the occasional external critic, could paralyze me at any step. My failures and successes have been felt acutely. Post-traumatic leadership is full of failures. Post-traumatic leadership is full of successes. Post-traumatic leadership is effective when you are engaged in mission, even missions with little chance of success. It is difficult and I know I will continue to have difficult days, that there will always be the imagined critics and the very real critics to tally my shortcomings. But, then again, what's the worst thing they can do to me? Cut off my hair and send me to Iraq?

Post-Traumatic Reconciliation

I treat the beat like it's a reverend/I tell the truth like father forgive me these are all my confessions.
—Sean Anderson, "Big Sean," in "Blessings"

What can we do to help veterans?" is a question I hear every time I speak. It implies a great deal. First, it assumes a "we." It assumes that a group of people, like a church, will be able to do something for veterans. It also assumes they need help. Many veterans, for example, struggle with suicidal thoughts. The first person to kill himself by jumping off the Golden Gate Bridge was Harold Wobber, a World War I veteran suffering from shell shock. The risk of suicide for WWI veterans was high and attested to in the literature born in that war.

Some reports indicate that twenty-two veterans kill themselves every day. One of the soldiers in my unit in Iraq killed himself. The shame, anger, and confusion that flooded me after his death still linger with me. I was responsible, after all, for keeping the unit suicide-free. His death was my moral injury. I could have—should have—done more, or so I tell myself in the dark watches of the night.

We want to help veterans. As I have stated above, we are all in this together. Even if you did not vote for the president or congress that involved us in the war, you are still in on it. We participate in war as a nation and it affects everything we do. Dr. Martin Luther King touched on this theme of interconnectedness in what was to be his last sermon on this earth. Just days before he was assassinated, he delivered a lengthy sermon on numerous topics. He spoke out against the Vietnam War. He denounced our rampant spending on war. We spend $500,000 to kill one North Vietnamese soldier, he said, yet we spend only $53 on a poor person in this country. He called for all of us to live together as brothers or we will perish together as fools. We listened, and then we forgot. His words still echo in that stone cathedral and out into the world.

We want to help veterans, but we do not always know how to help. What is help anyway but meeting a need? I do not like to be helped. I like to do things myself, solve things myself, and fix things myself. Normally, this works. But there are times I need help. I have described some of those times above. Veterans only need help when they need it, and like most of us, resent unasked-for help.

What can the Church do? First, stop helping. Second, listen to the veterans who are already inside the community. If the New Testament is a post-traumatic book written by post-traumatic people, then the Church is a post-traumatic community. Our whole ethos is devoted to learning to live post-trauma. Post-traumatic people struggle with trust. I know I did.

When I left active duty, I lost my ability to make friends. I moved to a new town in Kentucky. The only people I knew there were my ex-wife, her husband, and my two sons. That is not a good network upon which to build a social circle. I joined a church, a running club, a gym, but I did not have any friends. Friendship requires mutuality and trust. I had a hard time trusting anyone who did not serve with me. There was something about the army that gave me the ability to trust the people in it. Outside of that circle, I could never be sure if they would be there for me.

It makes sense. Post-traumatic people expect more trauma. We form alliances to mitigate the affects of that trauma. Those people should be able to deal with it. It is difficult to tell if civilians can handle such things, at least that is what I thought at the time. When I moved to Texas, I started over again. I made the acquaintance of a neighbor, a fellow student at the Seminary of the Southwest. And even though I was social, I did not have friends. But one Memorial Day everything changed.

A contact in Washington, DC, got in touch with me to discuss the Memorial Day concert on the National Mall. She was one of the producers of that event and wanted to know if I knew anyone who might be a good fit for the dramatic portion of the program. I recommended she feature Earl Granville, a wonderful veteran. Earl's story encompasses so many deep topics. War, suicide, his own injuries in Iraq—they were all part of the story. When Memorial Day finally arrived, I coordinated with my neighbor to watch it on his TV since I did not have one.

It was so moving I wept through the whole thing. I was sobbing out of control as I thought about the war in Iraq and Afghanistan, Earl's twin brother's suicide, and Earl's own amputation over there. When it was over I staggered out to the porch. There was my neighbor. He could tell I was having some big feelings. I hugged him, not hiding my sorrow, and he hugged me back. After that, I trusted him because he saw that part of me. Like Jesus, he saw me as I really was, and he loved me.

Seeing "that" part of a veteran is important. There will always be a part of us that is still "over there." Coming home takes a long time, and many of us are not home yet, by any means.

When I started the Episcopal Veterans Fellowship in Austin, Texas, I knew it would be tough. I knew it would be difficult to build a community of trust with a group of people who did not trust anyone. So, we started small. Our expectations changed with our experiences, and a solid group emerged. Trust happened when we shared our stories, our setbacks, and our successes.

Veterans do not need more barbeques, picnics, or trips to amusement parks. These are all very nice and I have enjoyed most of them. What we do need is community, connection to ourselves, each other, and to God. In my view, the Church is the best organization to do this.

Moral injury disrupts the connections in a veteran's life. The memories of things done and left undone paralyze many, causing withdrawal, conflict, and disconnection. One veteran in our group described his moral injury by telling a story about Vietnam. He told us how his unit would drive to a loading area to pick up supplies every morning. As a precaution, they would fire their machine guns into a field of thick banana trees just to make sure the enemy was not in a concealed position from which to ambush them. One morning, they found the body of a young boy they had killed. He was in the wrong place at the wrong time. The soldiers were just doing their job protecting the convoy. Who knows whose bullet actually struck him? It was Vietnam. In spite of all that, they had killed a child. He had killed a child. Due to the chaos of war, it is impossible to avoid collateral damage, but that knowledge does not mean participants, perpetrators of violence, accidental or on purpose, will not feel something. That something is moral injury.

The Church has been dealing with moral injury since its beginning. Peter's betrayal and restoration is one such example. The sacrament of reconciliation is the most concentrated form of healing from moral injury in the Episcopal Church. We bring the things we have done and the things we have left undone to the priest and hear God's forgiveness declared over us. This sacrament's liturgy is preserved in the Book of Common Prayer. The liturgy, the repetition, the written prayers allow the penitent to fully participate in the rite, as well as fully concentrate on the moral injury that was done.

Every Sunday morning, and other times in the week, the Church confesses its sins in the Prayer Book liturgy. The absolution in the Service of Holy Eucharist is just as effective as the absolution in the one-on-one encounter with the priest or confessor. For a time, we conducted several Pilgrimages of Remembrance and Reconciliation in Central Texas. Eight parishes participated and many found reconciliation. For the confession, we would write out our moral injuries, placing them in an "amnesty box," alluding to the box for any extra, saved rounds, grenades, or munitions. A deacon, usually Robert Chambers, would burn the paper confessions just outside the sanctuary. We could smell them burning. These were special times. I hope to participate in more of these healing services in the future.

Since beginning the Episcopal Veterans Fellowship, I have heard many confessions from veterans. While they are all sealed from disclosure, I can attest to how life changing the event was for the veterans and for me. I know the power of this sacrament firsthand. On one occasion I went to a local priest for the sacrament. I confessed my anger and my lack of forgiveness of my ex-wife. The burden of it was intolerable. I did not want to be angry forever. The priest placed his hand over my head and I received absolution. I wept. From the outside looking in, nothing spectacular happened.

Later that day I went to pick up my kids for the weekend. As my son opened the door of his mother's house, something unusual happened. Their dog did not bark at me. This was unusual, because she always did. Dogs, children, and a few adults can sense anger. Tillich described depression as "rage spread thin." For years, I spread my rage thin, but, on that day, I had given it to God. A little less of it was there. I think the dog knew it.

My anger at my ex-wife only damaged me. The angrier I was at her, the angrier I became at everyone. As I drew closer to reconciliation, as I experienced the forgiveness of God and the love demonstrated in the life, death, and resurrection of Jesus, the closer I drew to my ex-wife. When I embraced my own acceptance by God, I was able to see more of her humanity, wounded by the same war that wounded me. Wounded people are not safe; they can be dangerous as they act out their pain on the world. I certainly was after Iraq.

The closer I moved toward seeing my ex-wife as a complex human person, the further I was able to move away from her. I found I was no longer locked in a competitive struggle with her to win. I no longer feared losing to her. The win/lose dichotomy was beginning to crack. For me, this came from God's power to love and heal, not from my own willpower or inner strength.

I realize this was not some huge, monumental achievement, but one of many small steps toward reconciliation and healing after war. Veterans have to take the first step, no matter how small. One way to take steps, literally and metaphorically, is on pilgrimage.

Post-Traumatic Pilgrimage

"Where are you legs?" "I forgot them."
—Adele Levine in a conversation with an amputee patient in
*Run, Don't Walk: The Curious and Chaotic Life of a Physical
Therapist at Walter Reed Army Medical Center*

War has been with humanity since the dawn of time and is likely to stay. Wars, small and great, spring up around the world at irregular intervals. Wars are fought by human beings, mostly young human beings. While their experiences all differ, several unifying experiences are shared by all of war's participants.

The first unifying experience is propaganda. Warriors are inundated with notices from their own government that a particular war is necessary for survival. The enemy must be dehumanized and seen as a relentless threat that will consume our way of life.

A second unifying experience is love. When young men and women share the frightening horrors of death and destruction in war, they form close emotional bonds with each other. These bonds are seen in a soldier's disregard for his own safety while he rescues his buddy under fire. This love is seen in the nostalgia for war that lingers years after the conflict is over. This love can also be seen in the shattering grief, or survivor guilt, that too often results in self-destruction and suicide after homecoming.

A third unifying experience in warrior communities is participation in violence. Relatively few combatants kill in war, either in ancient or modern wars. Dave Grossman's *On Killing* demonstrates the natural human reluctance to kill. Direct killing in war by infantry is statistically rare. In World War II, only fourteen percent of U.S. personnel in Europe were in the infantry. This small group of men did suffer seventy percent of the casualties, however. The heavy psychological toll of direct infantry combat can be seen in the little-known statistic that ninety percent of the deserters at the Loire, France, military prison during World War II were from combat infantry companies. Participation in violence always has an effect. The severity of the effect varies, but it is generally classed into the overlapping worlds of post-traumatic stress disorder and moral injury.

The psychological community has reacted to recent combat trauma from Iraq and Afghanistan by researching treatment modalities for PTSD. The Veterans Administration has dedicated millions of dollars and personnel to this pursuit. Much good has come of these efforts, but not all combat trauma results in PTSD. Sometimes combat trauma produces moral injury.

The emerging study of moral injury from combat trauma demonstrates how the psychological community may not be able to fully address veterans who suffer this way. Perhaps moral theology offers a better way to understand and treat moral injury. This is the suggestion of Warren Kinghorn, who argues that moral and penitential theology and practice can provide the context for healing that combat veterans desperately need. The spiritual practice of pilgrimage fits better with moral and penitential theology than it does in the psychological community.

Pilgrimage can contribute to healing the invisible wounds caused by these three unifying features of war: propaganda, love, and participation in violence. Pilgrimage is as old as human history, since it is simple and requires only a spiritual destination and a way to get there. Most religious traditions practice pilgrimage in some form or another. Islam and

Hinduism have numerous pilgrimages with global participation. The ancient Jews went "Up to Jerusalem" every year, all the while chanting the Psalms. Pilgrimage in other religions is a worthwhile direction for further research, and finding combat veterans on pilgrimage in other religions would be even more fruitful. Ed Tick is reviving ancient pilgrimage practices for veterans. He leads pilgrimages to Asklepian healing shrines with amazing results. Many of these sites are now sites of Orthodox churches, a detail Tick draws attention to in his work.

During the Middle Ages, returning combat veterans would be excluded from the sacrament of Holy Eucharist until they made a penitential pilgrimage. The Knight, in Chaucer's *The Canterbury Tales,* is one such pilgrim. He had just come back from his campaign, and was on his way to make his pilgrimage. Although the Knight is both valiant and meek, his pilgrimage is mandatory. Other veteran pilgrimages in the Middle Ages were for specific acts of war, such as those done by a nobleman, Fulk Nerra, Count of Anjou. He embarked on a pilgrimage in the year 1,000 after feeling "the fear of Gehenna." He had recently been involved in the battle of Conquereuil, where it was said he had slaughtered many Bretons. Bernard Verkamp's *The Moral Treatment of Returning Warriors in Early Medieval and Modern Times* details the rigors of penance that medieval warriors were subject to upon their return from combat. It lists pilgrimage as one of the proscriptions to follow to attain this penance.

Rites of purification are attested in every warrior civilization. The ancient Hebrews had such rites, as detailed in the Torah (Numbers 31:19–24):

[Moses said:] "Camp outside the camp seven days; whoever of you has killed any person or touched a corpse, purify yourselves and your captives on the third and on the seventh day. You shall purify every garment, every article of skin, everything made of goats' hair, and every article of wood."

Eleazar the priest said to the troops who had gone to battle: "This is the statute of the law that the Lord has commanded Moses: gold, silver, bronze, iron, tin, and lead—everything that can withstand fire, shall be passed through fire, and it shall be clean. Nevertheless it shall also be purified with the water for purification; and whatever cannot withstand fire, shall be passed through the water. You must wash your clothes on the seventh day, and you shall be clean; afterward you may come into the camp."

By the Middle Ages, rites of purification were transmitted to the monumental sacramental system of the Roman Catholic Church. The sacrament of reconciliation, often called "confession," allowed the penitent to gain access to the sacraments. A pilgrimage was an enacted confession: a person traveled, a word etymologically connected to "travail," to a place of healing and restoration. It was supposed to be difficult and many pilgrimages were enacted "discalced" (barefoot) or carrying crosses or heavy loads.

More recent literature on the sacrament of reconciliation emphasizes healing and wholeness as the end state of the sacrament. In fact, Eugene Bianchi's *Reconciliation: The Function of the Church* holds forth that the sacrament restores the penitent to a state of *shalom*. For combat veterans, *shalom*, Hebrew for "peace," is the desired state of existence, but so difficult to find.

As the penitential system crumbled in the Reformation, fewer and fewer veterans made pilgrimages. In our modern society, veterans undergo some pilgrimages, such as the annual "Warriors to Lourdes" pilgrimage hosted in America by the Knights of Columbus. This pilgrimage has been active for fifty-seven years and draws military pilgrims from many different nations. It differs from the pilgrimages of the Middle Ages in that it primarily involves plane and automobile travel. No one walks. Perhaps this is why so few Americans do it.

Other secular pilgrimages occur in our society. Marathons, "Tough Mudder" obstacle races, and the "GORUCK Challenge" move the veteran from point "A" to point "B" under their own power. These are spiritual events, to be sure, since they bring meaning to people who participate. They do not, however, address the need for the community to welcome the warrior back home after the rites of purification.

Post-Traumatic Pilgrimage Today

Met Jesus on pilgrimage, still walking.
                                            —Bishop Andy Doyle

When a young German army chaplain, Paul Tillich, marched off to World War I, he believed in "a nice God who would make everything turn out for the best." He was enthusiastic about participating in war, proof that the German propaganda machine had done its job well. In order to overcome our hesitation to kill our fellow humans, we must see the enemy as less than human and willing, and able to do us harm. Propaganda campaigns accomplish this feat: they inspire fear that a subhuman enemy will come to steal, rape, and kill those most dear to us. The truth of the propaganda lies with those who make it, and they are often found to be wrong after the war is over.

As World War I plunged Europe into carnage and chaos, Tillich wrote that he no longer recognized God and that he felt he was no longer alive. Somewhere between the beginning and the end of his war, he experienced a loss of faith in the propaganda. Soldiers who go to war fight "Japs," "Nips," "Huns," "Gooks," and "Hajis." During or after the war, however, warriors often discover the humanity of their enemy. This realization that the warrior was killing men who were just like him leads to a shattering of trust in the authorities that authorized and encouraged the war.

Paul Reed found this out when he finally read a handwritten book of Vietnamese poems he found in a Vietcong lieutenant's backpack. For years he assumed the lieutenant was dead, most likely from Paul's own hand. After translating the poems into English, he discovered his enemy's humanity, which led him to rediscover his own humanity. In subsequent years, he located the author, who was miraculously still alive, and visited him in Vietnam. The book describes how Paul, a young paratrooper, was motivated to kill the Vietcong by the propaganda he heard in his community and in the Army. The propaganda made Paul an effective soldier, but it made him an ineffective man when he came home. His major symptom was numbness, a common experience of combat veterans. His numbness manifested itself in isolation that destroyed relationships until he finally opened the book of poetry and began his long pilgrimage home from war.

The shared experience of propaganda creates feelings of betrayal and detachment in combat veterans when they return home. Jonathan Shay writes about how ancient Greek warriors' feelings of betrayal by the gods are analogous to American Vietnam veterans' betrayal by the "American power holders." When a warrior becomes a political pawn, the feelings of betrayal cause deep spiritual wounds. Shay's second book, *Odysseus in America: Combat Trauma and the Trials of Homecoming,* describes in detail how alienated and distant combat veterans become after the war is over. Using Odysseus' long journey home from the Trojan War as a metaphor for today's combat veterans, the main description of a veteran is one who wanders in desolate and dangerous places.

Wandering is walking, but without a destination. Pilgrimage always has a destination. Celtic Christians called these destinations "thin places." These were places where heaven and earth seemed to meet. The spiritual practice of pilgrimage addresses this alienation that combat veterans face by giving them a destination. Pilgrimage sites are always fixed places.

They are often believed to be places "where miracles once happened, still happen, and may happen again."

The miracle that veterans need is the miracle of reconciliation. This miracle is a sacrament in the Roman Catholic, Lutheran, Orthodox, and Anglican traditions of Christianity. The sacrament of reconciliation recognizes the alienation of the one seeking reconciliation, the penitent. In the Book of Common Prayer the penitent says to the priest, I "have wandered far in a land that is waste." In the spiritual practice of pilgrimage, wanderers become pilgrims. This does not solve their problems or heal them instantly, but it does put them into a liminal state in between one's past and future.

The word "liminal" comes from the Latin *limin,* a threshold. Stepping over this threshold, the pilgrim enters a world of unforeseen possibilities. One of these possibilities might be a restoration of trust in the gods or the powers that sent him to war with their propaganda.

The biblical David loved Jonathan. The saga of their relationship begins and ends in constant battle and war. David's words about Jonathan ring true for countless combat veterans who experience the force that keeps them going in combat: "Jonathan lies slain upon your high places. I am distressed for you, my brother Jonathan; greatly beloved were you to me; your love to me was wonderful, passing the love of women" (2 Samuel 1:26).

Larry Dewey writes about a Marine rifleman who says, "In war, loyalties shrink down past country and family to one or two men who will be with you." The shared experience of love in war brings about profound grief when a buddy dies. Dewey's years of experience with combat veterans eventually led him to the conclusion that "fear does not cause men to break down nearly as often as broken hearts do." Grief must be numbed to keep combatants in battle. This has devastating consequences when the war is over and the veteran comes home. Numbness is often seen as a symptom of PTSD, and it is. However, numbness caused by grief cannot be treated the same way the numbness of PTSD is treated.

Perhaps pilgrimage offers hope for those who suffer from grief, which is also complicated by feelings of "survivor guilt." Transitions, as William

Bridges writes, always begin with an ending. An ending like death is the biggest ending of all. After the ending, for those who survived there is a wilderness or middle state that is difficult to endure. During this phase of a transition, humans feel immense anxiety and want to escape the middle state. This is counterproductive. Shelly Rambo and others compare this impatience with our impatience on Holy Saturday. After Good Friday, we want to skip directly to Easter. But Holy Saturday demands we wait with Jesus in the tomb. A walking pilgrim cannot rush, but must take each step after the last step. Pilgrimage offers a way for a combat veteran to slow down after Good Friday and wait on Holy Saturday for Easter to come.

Pilgrimage in the Middle Ages, like grief in any age, was hard. Roads were in disrepair and pilgrims were often robbed. In the mountain passes, pilgrims could only average about six miles per day. At this slow pace, grief has a chance to heal. Origen wrote in his *Exhortation to Martyrdom,* "Understand, then, if you can, what the pilgrimages of the soul are, especially when it laments with groaning and grief that it has been on pilgrimage so long." Only when a person arrives does one discover the meaning of the journey. Meaning-making takes time and contemplation. The physical activity of pilgrimage gives a grieving combat veteran that time in abundance.

For combat veterans with PTSD, eye movement desensitization and reprocessing (EMDR) therapy helps them heal psychologically from their trauma. The therapy is the leading evidence-based treatment for PTSD. In short, it combines techniques of "dual stimulation" that often keeps the client's eyes moving back and forth. This can also be done with tones or taps. While this is happening, the client processes the traumatic event. Over several sessions, the negative emotions associated with traumatic events are reduced.

Francine Shapiro discovered this therapy while she was walking and thinking about a particularly troubling situation in her life. As she walked, she noticed the troubling memory disappeared. She continued to walk around the duck pond and noticed a shift in her eye movement. Hence, EMDR was born! In spite of discovering this psychological phenomenon while walking, EMDR patients in treatment rarely, if ever, walk while they process their traumatic events. Were medieval pilgrims practicing a primitive form of EMDR as they hiked along the duck ponds of Europe to holy shrines? Who can know? What we do know is that in the medieval health care system, this was the primary prescription for combat veterans.

The effect of killing on the killer is profound. Warren Kinghorn calls it the "human cost of war." The cost to the one killed is obvious, but the cost to the person doing the killing, the killer, is more difficult to unravel. As noted above, very few combatants directly kill another human in war. However, most of the participants in war observe killing and its aftermath. Furthermore, perpetrating violence or failing to prevent violent events produces moral injury. Numerous studies show that persons who kill in war are much more likely to commit suicide and fall into a host of other self-destructive behaviors. The high suicide rate among veterans has risen in recent years. The Veterans Administration reports twenty-two suicides by veterans per day. The real number may be higher, since some states with large veteran populations like Texas refuse to report their veteran suicides.

Killing an enemy combatant in war is in the job description of every warrior. Killing noncombatants in war, or killing the enemy under morally dubious conditions, is not. The suffering of those who do this is profound. All wars produce numerous opportunities for "collateral damage," the phrase used to describe almost every noncombatant killing in war. This is the primary place where PTSD stops and moral injury begins. If PTSD is a fear response that marks the brain, moral injury from killing the innocent, or even another live human, is more akin to the theological concepts of sin and guilt.

This is precisely why the spiritual practice of pilgrimage can address issues of sin and guilt. "We begin our pilgrimage with a call to repentance," writes Alan Jones in his classic *Passion for Pilgrimage.* Pilgrims in the Middle Ages were instructed to pay all their debts and make their wills before pilgrimage, as if preparing for death. The entire structure of the medieval pilgrimage, "the medieval journey to God," existed to deal with sin and guilt.

Ignatius of Loyola, whom we met earlier, served as a soldier and found his religious calling while he was recovering from injuries received in combat. His first act after his recovery was to embark on a pilgrimage to Jerusalem. His confession took him three days to complete. He set out to start a new life, dressed as a poor beggar-pilgrim. His penance soon became more extreme. He let his hair grow wild and his fingernails became filthy. He wore sackcloth and confessed his sins weekly. This pilgrimage to Jerusalem became the inspiration of the *Spiritual Exercises*. Ignatius bridged the gap between the medieval world and the modern world, but his practice of pilgrimage made the leap with him. The *Spiritual Exercises* offer a plan for repentance, encompassing every area of life. The eradication of sin can still be found on the pilgrim's road.

The famous pilgrimage to St. James of Compostela still contains the pile of rocks symbolizing the burdens of sin left behind on the journey. This is evidence that modern humanity has not completely lost its sense of sin and repentance. The road to forgiveness is a long one. In Luke 10, Jesus sends his seventy followers out to walk from village to village. They are to walk without sandals, a painful prospect in any age. When they return, Jesus praises their mighty works, even though their main work was simply walking from place to place. The next parable Jesus tells is of the Good Samaritan, a parable about the perils of the journey and the grace we find when we are beat up and left for dead.

The Protestant classic, *Pilgrim's Progress*, embodies more of the medieval quest for God than its characters or readers readily admit. It begins with the vision of "a man clothed with rags, standing in a certain place, with his face from his own house, a book in his hand, and a great burden on his back." Although the theology of the 1678 book is decidedly Puritan, the practice is thoroughly medieval. While medieval pilgrimages were obsessed with visiting saints' relics, pilgrimages in the Reformation were more focused on the removal of sin by finding justification by God. The practice, however, remained unchanged.

An ancient Celtic prayer of pilgrimage begins, "May God free me from my wickedness/May God free me from my entrapment." Combat veterans who killed an enemy often experience a moral injury that feels like "wickedness," in spite of their killing being justified by the law of war. There is also guilt from "standing by" while noncombatants die. Ron Capps writes about the frustration of inaction in his memoir *Seriously Not Alright: Five Wars in Ten Years.* In spite of Capps's repeated attempts to bring military intervention to the genocides of Kosovo, the genocides still happened. When he visited the mass graves, his first thought was "Yellow. Their skin was yellow." This image of war dead stays with him to this day. This and other memories of "standing by" led to severe PTSD symptoms such as tics, anxiety, inability to focus, shaking of the hands, hyper vigilance, panic attacks, and quickness to anger. His "craziness" would show him "pictures on the big screen" of his mind. He would curl into a ball and rock back and forth on the floor, shaking uncontrollably. The downward spiral continued until he received psychological help for PTSD from the Veterans Administration. How much of Capps's struggle was moral injury and how much was PTSD? One can never know. What we can know is what he wrote near the end of his book:

> Mine is moral cowardice: failing to take action to protect survivors. . . . It has seemed to me at times that it was the mere memory of ten years of failure, of weakness, of all the dead I did not save, that broke my mind. Were I more religious, I would call these sins of omission rather than sins of commission.

Capps describes his book as a "confession" and he frames his feelings and symptoms in religious terms of sins of omission and sins of commission. While he makes it clear he is not religious, could a religious solution help him, even a little? Pilgrimage is religious, but it differs from many religious disciplines since it asks more of the body than the mind or soul. Like pilgrimage, ancient paganism was not "heavily theorized" like Christianity. Therefore, the accessibility and universality of pilgrimage transcends theoretical constructs of religion. There are few articles of faith required to walk to a shrine, and as Martin Sheen's film, "The Way" suggests, even skeptical pilgrims can discover a rekindling of faith on the road.

If combat veterans have broken the "Geneva Convention of the soul," their guilt is increased exponentially. "Breaking the Geneva Convention of the soul" is what Larry Dewey calls acts of violence that contradict one's own ethical or moral beliefs. They usually involve killing a noncombatant suspected of being a combatant. Religious rituals, like pilgrimage, create the conditions where these feelings of wickedness and entrapment can be expiated and dissolved.

Perhaps this is part of the function of some biblical miracles of healing. Many of them involve the supplicant walking somewhere for healing. Proud Naaman must journey to Palestine from Aramea for healing (2 Kings 5). When he arrives he is told to go immerse himself in the Jordan River. He comes back healed. Jesus tells ten lepers to go show themselves to the priest (Matthew 8). They go, and only one makes the return pilgrimage to thank Jesus. If nothing more, these stories demonstrate that part of the miracle is the trip to the miracle, as well as the trip back to the place of origin. All of life, including miracles, is pilgrimage. How we go seems to be just as important as where we go in our spiritual journeys.

The longest pilgrimage I ever embarked on almost broke me. Shortly after I left active duty in the army, I moved to Kentucky. During my ten months there, I would frequently run long distances, often from my apartment to Lincoln's birthplace, about fifteen miles away. I would run out there early in the morning and stand for a few moments on the thirty-sixth step of his shrine. The shrine there has fifty-six steps on it, one for each year of the president's life. I was thirty-six at the time, and it was not a long way to the top of the stairs from there.

I would run back as the day heated up. I would think about life, death, the army, and everything. During these runs, I learned I could run long distances. This led me to plan the long running pilgrimage. Since I was to be ordained to the priesthood in June 2012, I planned to run from Springfield, Illinois, to Washington, DC. This was because I was being ordained by the Bishop of Springfield, The Rt. Rev. Daniel Martins. The ceremony, however, was to take place in Washington, DC. Yes, I know, it's complicated.

After serving at the altar that Sunday (I was a deacon at the time), I was blessed by the Ven. Shawn Denney, archdeacon of the Diocese of Springfield. Then I ran out of the church and headed east. It took me eighteen days to complete the pilgrimage. I would run all day, stopping after sundown at any motel I could find along Route 40. Once, there wasn't a hotel so I just kept moving forward through the night. All I carried with me was a paper map and a credit card. Sometimes, if the motel had a guest computer, I would check my route on Google Maps or call my friend, Kurt, who would search for a good stopping point on his computer.

Since I was worried about not arriving in time, I hastened my journey by buying a single-speed bicycle in Zanesville, Ohio. After two days, my right knee began to hurt from pedaling up some seriously steep hills. Soon, I was jogging the bike up the hills and coasting down the other side. After two and a half days on the bike, I abandoned it at a bike rack and continued to run. I arrived in Washington on the Wednesday before my Sunday ordination.

During those eighteen days, I experienced serious pain in my legs as I adjusted to the relentless running. The cumulative effect of thirty, forty, or more miles a day would leave my legs twitching and spasming all night, waking me every hour. My feet swelled up about two sizes so I bought bigger shoes on a rainy day in Columbus. But that was the easy part. The difficult part was the silence and the solitude. As cars whizzed by me on old Route 40, I was alone with my thoughts. Without any human conversation day after day, my mind played songs over and over again. I also started to remember things. Some of the things were happy, but most of the memories were events I had forgotten for safety reasons.

I would remember long conversations with my ex-wife in which I, ever so subtly, spoke condescendingly to her during the early days of our marriage. I remembered how controlling I had been with her, how unhelpful I had been with our two sons, and how this contributed to the breakdown of our marriage. These memories were so vivid I found myself weeping with regret for how I treated her during those days.

I also remembered how I acted after Iraq and after the divorce. I remembered how I took the wooden cradle my brother made for the birth of my baby sister and threw it off the back of a truck into the dump. I had just moved it, disassembled, from Pennsylvania, to Texas, to Washington State, and then to its final resting place in Northern Virginia. My first two sons had slept in it and I had hoped for a third to grace it. When the divorce loomed large, I knew this was not to be. I pitched it off the back of the truck, like it was a used pizza box. A few years later my brother asked me if I could send it to him, since they were having another baby. I told him what I had done, and even then the anger I had in the moment kept me from feeling anything. But out here, on my own, with no distractions, I could see the beautiful wooden pieces land on a great heap of old washers and dryers, never to be seen again.

After several days of these memories, it became terrifying to be alone with my thoughts like this. There was nothing to be distracted by, nothing to switch the channel of my mind. I had to face reality. Facing reality is always difficult for me. The terror only subsided when I started to give these memories to God, begging God to forgive me for my misuse of power and my blindness to the needs of others. Pilgrimage offers us the opportunity to face reality, but giving memories to God is not easy in the anxiety of the moment.

In order to give these memories to God I had to create a calm space in my mind. I first learned how to do this on the rifle range at the Marine Corps Recruit Depot, Parris Island, South Carolina. As a nineteen-year-old recruit I learned how to breathe. I learned to breathe in, and let it out until I could feel that drop at the bottom of the breath. That is the moment you pull the trigger. I learned it almost perfectly that summer, and qualified as an Expert Rifleman. I shot ten man-sized targets at five hundred yards with open sights. I could barely even see the target, but I hit him ten times. Now, years later, I was trying to hit life's targets, some closer and some at five hundred yards. That breathing calmed me down.

It settled me to where I could be absolutely calm—calm enough to hit the target. On this pilgrimage I found myself returning to this practice out of necessity. Breathing offers the human organism a rare chance to control our involuntary physical responses. It does, after all, cross the voluntary and involuntary. By breathing this way I was able to create some space to pray, if I had not been already.

Episcopal churches, among others, have pilgrimage in their DNA. Many feast days called for long processions in times past. Pilgrimages to England and the Holy Land could also be designed for post-traumatic veteran pilgrims on their way home from war. Churches can train veterans to be vergers and commission them to lead the church in processions and pilgrimages.

As I write these words, Air Force veteran and Episcopalian Christian Ken Meyer, is wrapping up his six-hundred-plus-mile "Never Quit March for PTS Awareness." Ken's parish church, Holy Comforter in Spring, Texas, along with his priest, the Rev. Jimmy Abbot, have been very supportive of him. Communities across Texas have attended events along his route and even walked with him for some of the miles. It is hoped that this pilgrimage will be come more and more common for veterans in days to come.

In November 2015, I was honored to preach at the national cathedral on their Sunday observance of Veterans Day. While I was there I was reminded by Ruth Frey, the cathedral's director of programs, that the eastern steps of the cathedral are called the Pilgrims Steps. When the cathedral was designed, pilgrims were expected to walk up those steps and into the cathedral. My dream is for five, fifty, or maybe even five hundred veterans to one day walk up those steps together on our long journey home from war.

My first and last word for the post-traumatic community, the Church, is to start something. That first "something" is prayer. Lynn Smith-Henry and I prayed in the Seminary of the Southwest library for a community of Christian veterans to be born. You can do this too. This is at the heart of our new monastic Christian community, the Hospitallers of St. Martin.

Hospitallers were monks who accompanied pilgrims on pilgrimage and helped wounded warriors after battle. St. Martin is the patron saint of veterans who gave of himself for the poor and vulnerable and brought reconciliation and healing during and after war.

We hope this Christian community can grow and provide a leadership corps for veterans' ministry in the United States and the world. The first task of the community is *prayer*. We pray the daily office and fast periodically to intensify our devotional and prayer life. The second task is *hospitality*. This is done as we welcome veterans into our groups and fellowship. It can be done in the waiting area at the VA hospital. It can happen anywhere. The third task in our Rule of Life is *reconciliation*. Each of our members is an expert in reconciliation. We practice it ourselves and offer it to others. The sacrament of reconciliation in the Book of Common Prayer can be led by anyone, priest or layperson. Special instructions are given for both presiders, and any baptized Christian can do it. The world needs this and the Hospitallers of St. Martin are moving out, following Jesus into the world.

Post-Traumatic Compline

But they urged [Jesus] strongly, saying, "Stay with us, because it is almost evening and the day is now nearly over."

—Luke 24:29

In typical Episcopalian fashion, our evening Episcopal Veterans Fellowship groups end with Compline. The progression of the meetings moves from a time of check-in, to a short teaching, to the presentation of a lament (turning experience into art), and then Compline. This works because we generally move from the surface of our lives to deeper and deeper places as the meetings progress. Rarely is there much vulnerability in the check-in, although this has happened occasionally. During the teaching portion, one of the participants will share a difficult experience that relates to the topic. When we get to the time of lament, the emotional temperature often goes up. Unresolved conflict from forty years ago can manifest in the present. Arguments with superior officers, played out in the mind for a decade, are still fresh. The loss of good friends and the moral injuries of war and homecoming often reappear.

Since we are not group therapy or formal psychology, our interventions are different from what you may find in another, more clinical setting. In

Episcopal Veterans Fellowship meetings, when some rather intractable, unresolvable, unforgiveable, situations come up, we pray. The prayers we pray at this time are found in the office of Compline.

Normally, when I am facilitating the meeting, I find a pause and say something like, "Wow, Stephanie, you really put a lot out there." I open it up for a time for the group to affirm or show some love, and then I say, "Let's go take that to God."

We shuffle up to the chapel, where we light the candles, open our Prayer Books to page 127, and begin. Compline is the final night office in the Book of Common Prayer, a service that comes to us from the monastic communities that prayed seven offices per day. Since its inclusion in the 1979 Prayer Book, the office has experienced a resurgence in the Episcopal Church. Youth groups, vestries, and other gatherings pray the seven-minute service to conclude a day or meeting. The book, *Prayer as Night Falls: Experiencing Compline,* chronicles Compline's rise in popularity at St. Mark's Cathedral in 1956, shortly after World War II. The sung service at St. Mark's was founded by a World War II veteran, Peter Hallock.

Compline is how I became Episcopalian. During my first weeks at U.S. Army Chaplain School in Fort Jackson, South Carolina, Fr. Jeff Whorton, a fellow student, gathered us for Compline in his quarters. There were usually four of us, sometimes as many as twelve. We would pray it through. I found the written prayers difficult to pray, but I far preferred it to the rambling, free-flowing entreaties I was used to. Compline collected all our prayers into the written prayers—which is, of course, why they are called "collects."

We prayed these prayers every night, while the intensity of the Iraq war picked up. We knew where we were going. After our final field exercise, we collapsed, exhausted beyond measure, on the dirt floor of a large tent late one night. Because of light discipline, we had to keep things dark. Jeff started to pray Compline and we all joined in. In two months we had memorized it. Praying Compline in the dark was different, but it was also the same. It was as if God knew us in the dark. Soon we were deployed with our units. We would get to know our soldiers so well they would know our voice in the dark. God's presence is not confined to churches. Holy ground is everywhere.

The veterans gather in the holy ground of the chapel and pray the office. The prayers are all about threats of death and entreaties for protection. The opening sentence is, "The Lord Almighty grant us a peaceful night and a perfect end." A peaceful night means something to a warrior. Peace is not a state of mind. It is not the absence of war. It is those few moments in between the hell of war. The prayer is that this one night— just one—be peaceful. That is all we can ask for.

The confession is shorter than in the Sunday services, but it gets to the point. We have sinned and we have left things undone. The veterans carry their moral injuries, the things done and left undone. They have brought them here, to this place, to see if God forgives. The absolution comes, and they have been forgiven.

"O God, make speed to save us. O Lord, make haste to help us." Save, help, make haste—these are infantry terms. This is all you can hope for when you are pinned down and supplies are running low. The Psalms are all warriors' laments. They call on God to defend us. They call on God to be a refuge, a fortress, a castle. Psalm 91 is forever linked to warriors. "A thousand shall fall at your side." This promise was repeated by many soldiers in many wars. In my war, Iraq, someone distributed handkerchiefs with the entire psalm printed on one side. We put them in our helmets, hoping for the best. And here it is, in Compline, being prayed by warriors who are on the long journey home from war.

The remainder of the office continues to emphasize these themes. In war, night is not a time to rest, it is prime time for combat. It is when the advantages of a superior force can be mitigated. The dark is a great equalizer. Yes, Lord, keep us under the shadow of your wings.

"Guard us sleeping" is repeated twice at the end. Most veterans I know have trouble sleeping. We struggle with sleep, in spite of exhaustion.

We scroll through our phones, sharing memes of war and battle. PTSD memes abound, perhaps an attempt to show the world what is in our soul. But they do not see it, for they are asleep. Compline, an ancient practice, needs to be the standard operating procedure (SOP) for veterans who want to rest in peace, this night and forevermore.

Practical Steps toward Becoming a Post-Traumatic Church

But this too is true: stories can save us.
—Tim O'Brien in *The Things They Carried*

My life is living proof that the Church can make a difference in veterans' lives. I am thankful I met the post-traumatic God and I am thankful for the post-traumatic community that welcomed me with open, wounded arms. I am thankful I can carry the reconciling love of Jesus to the world. I am thankful for my time in Iraq. I am thankful for my divorce. I am thankful for the women and men who walked with me, who still walk with me on this journey home from war. I am thankful for everything, and the things I am not yet thankful for I hope to be some day. Look at your wounds and then look at the wounds of Jesus. Come and be grasped by his love, grounded in the ground of being, accepted by a God who appears when God disappears.

In this book I have attempted to use myself as an example of how veterans find healing and reconciliation after war. I realize that not everyone is like me. I have done so on Henry Stack Sullivan's hunch that we are more alike than we are different. I hope I have made it clear that there are no one-size-fits-all ways to care for veterans who have been to hell and back. I trust the Holy Spirit to lead you and your church into the ministry that will fit your gifts and talents. But, in the interest of practicality, here are steps to take to become a church that cares for veterans.

1. The post-traumatic spiritual care for veterans I offer up in this book is communal, theological, penitential, and liturgical. Chances are, your local parish is already doing one or all of these things. Begin with the assumption you already have the tools to do ministry.

2. Anglican theology has generally favored slow-growth spirituality over any quick-fix attempts at sanctification and reconciliation. Be patient with yourself and your community for that is what we are offering an impatient world.

3. Identify the veterans who have a passion for veterans' ministry. If you are that person, find a "battle buddy," a partner to pray with about the next step.

4. Identify veterans in your community. Veterans' organizations abound in all our communities. I am a member of Team RWB, and I have found great relationships there. Almost all of these organizations appreciate volunteers who are either veterans or supporters of veterans.

5. Keep making the connections. Look for clues that someone might be a veteran. Pins, hats, and bumper stickers are good places to start. Introduce them to veterans already in your parish.

6. Attend a conference about moral injury or PTSD.

7. Do not reinvent the wheel. Visit the Soul Repair Center's website at www.brite.edu/soulrepair and download their Moral Injury Meetings Guidebook. Use the Episcopal Veterans Fellowship's Five Stations curriculum (see page 133) in a group setting. Call a meeting of two or three veterans and start the conversation.

8. Ask your bishop if your diocese has an Episcopal Veterans Fellowship. If so, get in touch with them; if not, start one.
9. Start a book group and read this book.
10. Contact the Episcopal Veterans Fellowship for a speaker to come to your parish and share their story.
11. Organize a Memorial Day morning prayer service with a list of those who died from your parish or town.
12. Attend a Memorial Day ceremony at a local veterans' monument.
13. Never forget female veterans. They are often mistaken for military spouses.
14. Remind your pastor or priest of upcoming veterans' holidays and events like Veterans Day, Memorial Day, and the Commemoration of the Four Chaplains (February 3).
15. Read the books in the bibliography and start a Post-Traumatic Book Club.
16. Read books by veterans so that you can hear their stories firsthand.
17. Form a veterans panel and ask your pastor or priest to moderate it for Veterans Day.
18. Keep listening for it is the first task of love.

Five Stations on the Pilgrimage after War

*by David W. Peters and the founding members
of the Hospitallers of St. Martin*

*War is hell, but that's not the half of it, because war is also
mystery and terror and adventure and courage and discovery
and holiness and pity and despair and longing and love.
War is nasty; war is fun. War is thrilling; war is drudgery.
War makes you a man; war makes you dead.*
—Tim O'Brien, *The Things They Carried*

*Many will argue that there is nothing remotely spiritual in
combat. Consider this. Mystical or religious experiences have four
common components: constant awareness of one's own inevitable
death, total focus on the present moment, the valuing of other
people's lives above one's own, and being part of a larger religious
community such as the Sangha, ummah, or church. All four of
these exist in combat. The big difference is that the mystic sees
heaven and the warrior sees hell. Whether combat is the dark side
of the same version, or only something equivalent in intensity,
I simply don't know. I do know that at the age of fifteen I*

*had a mystical experience that scared the hell out of me and
both it and combat put me into a different relationship
with ordinary life and eternity.*

*Most of us, including me, would prefer to think of a sacred space
as some light-filled wondrous place where we can feel good and
find a way to shore up our psyches against death. We don't want
to think that something as ugly and brutal as combat could be
involved in any way with the spiritual. However, would any
practicing Christian say that Calvary Hill was not a sacred space?*
—Karl Marlantes, *What It Is Like to Go to War*

*Now on that same day two of them were going to a village
called Emmaus, about seven miles from Jerusalem, and talking
with each other about all these things that had happened.
While they were talking and discussing, Jesus himself came
near and went with them.*
—Luke 24:13–15

Veterans are men and women who survived war. While the trip home
from Iraq, Afghanistan, Kosovo, Vietnam, or any other conflict can
be measured in hours or days, the pilgrimage of war takes far longer.

During the medieval period, veterans returning from war often went on
penitential pilgrimages to find reconciliation after war. Most warrior cultures
have rituals and rites that restore the warrior to the community after war.

Will you consider this pilgrimage? Will you consider taking the first
step toward the first station on the way? It won't be easy and it may make
you uncomfortable at times. But know this, you are not alone. The warriors in this room are going to walk it with you, as well as the communion
of warrior saints that look down on us from above. Most importantly of
all, Jesus will walk with you, all the way to the end.

Group Rules

- Everyone is on his or her own pilgrimage and we cannot solve each other's problems. We take all the issues we raise in the group to the prayer time at the end.
- We give each other the gift of listening. No responses to comments or stories unless someone asks for a response.
- Confidentiality above all.
- Tell the truth about who you are.

Every meeting should begin with a lament. A lament is a work of art, a poem, song, object, or reading that captures the emotional experience of war. Group members are expected to bring something. Arrangements should be made prior to the group meeting about who is bringing what.

Station 1

Plan of Attack: The group leader shows how war grants the power of death to combatants. Historically, the power of death is in the domain of the gods, or God. This is why we say that war is fought in the mythical realm. When we participate in it, it participates in us. This can be illustrated on a chalkboard or whiteboard, if available.

So, what was it like in Vietnam, Iraq, Afghanistan, Bosnia? Few veterans can answer this question because words cannot entirely capture our experiences. Our reverence for our own experiences should not be cause for further withdrawal, however. We need to engage our experiences, for they are us and we are them.

The theological point to bring up here is Jesus's post-resurrection appearances. Jesus introduces himself by showing the scars on his hands and feet. Clearly, his body bore scars, but what of his mind and emotions? His torturous death must have existed in his memory and he *never* speaks of it to his disciples. There is much to ponder here and that is probably the best approach.

Questions (Remember, we all just listen!)

1. How much power did you or your unit have in war?
2. How did you participate in that power?

The group leader now discusses the symptoms of returning warriors:

1. Have you ever felt numb to what was going on around you?
2. Have you ever felt hyper-vigilant?
3. Have you ever had a violent outburst of anger, disproportionate to the situation?
4. Have any of these things affected your relationships?
5. How did you describe your experiences in combat to family and friends back home? How did that go?

The leader does not attempt to solve any of the problems. The leader leads the group in their Pilgrimage to God. Group members are encouraged to share these struggles during the confession or free intercessions of the Order for Compline.

The group concludes with moving to a suitable location to pray the Order for Compline on page 127 in the *Book of Common Prayer*.

Station 2

Plan of Attack: The group leader will attempt to show how war produces loss and loss produces grief. Veterans are often unaware of their own grief. Larry Dewey's *War and Redemption* identifies PTSD as a "grief issue." He came to this conclusion after spending thousands of hours with WWII and Vietnam veterans. Dewey shows in his book how we go to war because of propaganda (sometimes true, sometimes not). We stay in war, he argues, for love. We love the people who go into the fire with us. We form deep attachments to them and they to us. The loss of one of these people is often a greater loss than losing a biological family member. There are obvious losses like the death of a battle buddy, and less obvious losses like the loss of safety, identity, or relationship. Everyone loses something in a war and it is always a surprise.

Questions (Just listen, no solving!):

1. What were some of the reasons you went to war?
2. Who were some of the people with whom you built a strong friendship?
3. Did anyone say you were different when you came back from military service or war? In what way?
4. What were your losses in war (financial, relational, spiritual, physical)?

After everyone has shared, the leader leads the group in their Pilgrimage to God. Group members are encouraged to share these struggles during the confession or free intercessions of the Order for Compline.

The group concludes with moving to a suitable location to pray the Order for Compline on page 127 in the *Book of Common Prayer*. Candles for the departed or for other losses can be lit.

Station 3

Plan of Attack: This group session will tackle the thorny issue of theodicy. Where was God when _____. If war is hell, is God in hell? Why didn't God prevent some or all of the deaths? Why did the good die young? The horrors and cruelty of war challenge the traditional Christian belief that God is in control of the universe.

For many, this is a theological and philosophical exercise. For veterans, this question can result in anger, feelings of betrayal, and a sense of abandonment. Anger at God is a sign of a strong relationship with God, as evidenced by the Old Testament prophets. The leader should work hard in this session to clear space for members to express their emotions without judgment.

Larry Dewey, mentioned at Station 2, also addresses what happens to people when they "Break the Geneva Convention of the Soul." That is, when they do something in war that they know to be wrong but are driven by circumstances to make a "lesser of two (or three) evils" decision. Warriors are often forced by circumstance to stand by while atrocities (large and small) happen before them. The result is often moral injury.

Questions (Don't solve, just listen.):

1. Where was God when _____?
2. How would you describe God's involvement in the world before you went to war?
3. How would you describe God's involvement in the world now?
4. How did Jesus confront this "Where was God question" during his earthly life? ("My God, my God, why have you forsaken me?")
5. Do any of the prayers or statements from Compline relate to your military service, or your current experience?

After everyone has shared, the leader leads the group in their Pilgrimage to God. Group members are encouraged to share these struggles during the confession or free intercessions of the Order for Compline.

The group concludes with moving to a suitable location to pray the Order for Compline on page 127 in the *Book of Common Prayer*.

Station 4

Plan of Attack: The last three stations focus on "what's wrong." These are necessary stations on the pilgrim's path, but they can be very difficult to process. The remaining two sessions focus on moving toward the light. At this station we ask ourselves the question, "What now?" What do I need to do for my own healing and health? What do I need to be honest about? What changes in my life do I need to make so I'm not stuck here forever?

The Scripture to examine for this is the story of the Philippian jailor (Acts 16:25–34). Philippi is a "Suicide Post." Cassius and Brutus killed themselves there after murdering Julius Caesar. Once the dishonor of lost prisoners is suspected, the jailor goes for his sword to kill himself. It is instinctive. Then, when he hears everything is not lost, he asks, "What must I do to be saved?" He and his family are baptized that night. What part of our baptismal vow do we need to renew at this time, after we return from war, a baptism in blood?

Questions (Let it be, let it be.):

1. Describe a veteran you know who seems to be healthy and doing "OK"? What are his or her qualities?
2. Is it OK to not be OK?
3. What helped me when I came home from war? What helps me now?
4. What difficult changes do I need to make to move toward healing?
5. What is holding me back from becoming healthier?

After everyone has shared, the leader leads the group in their Pilgrimage to God. Group members are encouraged to share these struggles during the confession or free intercessions of the Order for Compline.

The group concludes with moving to a suitable location to pray the Order for Compline on page 127 in the *Book of Common Prayer.*

Station 5

Plan of Attack: The leader will guide the pilgrims to confront the spiritual gifts given to us in war that we can use to prevent future wars, help others heal, and bring about more reconciliation in the world. A brief overview of certain biblical characters and saints may be appropriate. David the King was a warrior who made the building of the Temple possible. He also wrote most of the Psalms. St. Martin of Tours was a Roman cavalryman who became a monk and bishop. St. Francis of Assisi was a soldier and POW before starting a religious order. St. Ignatius of Loyola was a military officer who started a worldwide movement of evangelization and spiritual direction. Jürgen Moltmann was a German soldier and POW during World War II. He became a theologian whose most famous work is *A Theology of Hope.* The list goes on and on.

Lazarus, who had died, is brought back to life by Jesus. We wonder what it felt like to live again after going into the world of the dead. Veterans know what this is like. What will we do with our new life?

Questions (No advice unless it is asked for.):

1. Where do your gifts match up with what the world needs right now?
2. What can you do to lower the number of wars in the world?
3. Who else needs to make this pilgrimage?
4. What station do you need to return to before you complete this pilgrimage?

After everyone has shared, the leader leads the group in their Pilgrimage to God. Group members are encouraged to share these struggles during the confession or free intercessions of the Order for Compline.

The group concludes with moving to a suitable location to pray the Order for Compline on page 127 in the *Book of Common Prayer.*

APPENDIX: THE TWELVE STEPS

The Soul Repair Center at Brite Divinity School was founded in 2012 to research and better understand recovery from the trauma and moral injury of war. In the inaugural Soul Repair Center class in 2014, led by the Center's director, Rita Nakashima Brock, the group developed a manual, "Moral Injury Meeting: A Twelve-Step Program toward Recovery from Moral Injury for Veterans and Their Families and Friends." It includes the following twelve steps, which I have found helpful in Episcopal Veterans Fellowship meetings. The manual is available on the Soul Repair Center's website.

The Twelve Steps

1. We admitted we cannot change our experiences of war or the effects war has had on ourselves and on our family.
2. We believed that powers or a power greater than ourselves can restore us to wholeness.
3. We made the decision to turn our will and our lives over to the care of what we call sacred as we explore our core values and beliefs about our spiritual ground or higher power.
4. We made a searching and fearless moral inventory of ourselves.
5. We admitted to what we believe to be sacred, to ourselves, and to another human the exact nature of our injuries.
6. We're entirely ready to have powers greater than ourselves to aid us in healing and accepting ourselves and our injuries.

7. We humbly asked what we call sacred to remove our feelings of shame.

8. We made a list of all people we had harmed and are willing to make amends to them all.

9. We made direct amends to those people wherever possible, except when to do so would injure us or others, and we made direct amends to ourselves.

10. We continued to take personal inventory, and when we were wrong, promptly admitted it.

11. We sought through prayer and meditation to improve our relationship with what we hold sacred, praying or meditating for spiritual understanding and discernment of what is good and right in ourselves and for the power to carry that out.

12. Having had an inner awakening as the result of these steps, we tried to carry this message to others, and to practice these principles in all our affairs.

It is not necessary to achieve perfect adherence to these principles. We are not saints. The point is our willingness to grow along spiritual lines. The principles we have set down are guides to progress. We claim spiritual progress rather than spiritual perfection.

The Twelve Steps were created by the inaugural Soul Repair class at Brite Divinity School, taught by Rita Nakashima Brock.

BIBLIOGRAPHY

Bass, Diana Butler. *Grounded: Finding God in the World—A Spiritual Revolution.* San Francisco: HarperOne, 2015.

Basu, Moni. "Why Suicide Rate among Veterans May Be More than 22 a Day." http://www.cnn.com/2013/09/21/us/22-veteran-suicides-a-day/ (accessed April 2, 2016).

Bianchi, Eugene. *Reconciliation: The Function of the Church.* New York: Sheed and Ward, Inc., 1969.

Boudreau, Tyler. *Packing Inferno: The Unmaking of a Marine.* Port Townsend, WA: Feral House, 2008.

Nakashima Brock, Rita, and Gabriella Lettini. *Soul Repair: Recovering from Moral Injury after War.* Boston: Beacon Press, 2013.

Brown, Brené. *Daring Greatly: How the Courage to Be Vulnerable Transforms the Way We Live, Love, Parent, and Lead.* New York: Avery Press, 2012.

Capps, Ron. *Seriously Not All Right: Five Wars in Ten Years.* Tucson, AZ: Schaffner Press, 2013.

Carey, Dave. *The Way We Choose: Lessons for Life From a POW's Experience.* 2nd ed. Portland, OR: Arnica Creative Services, 2005.

Coleman, Simon, and John Elsner. *Pilgrimage: Past and Present in the World Religions.* Cambridge, MA: Harvard University Press, 1995.

Crimmins, Daniel. "You Grow Up Wanting to Be Luke Skywalker, Then Realize You've Become a Stormtrooper for the Empire." Accessed May 17, 2016. http://upriser.com/posts/you-grow-up-wanting-to-be-luke-skywalker-then-realize-you-ve-become-a-stormtrooper-for-the-empire.

Dewey, Larry. *War and Redemption: Treatment and Recovery in Combat-Related Traumatic Stress Disorder.* Surry, UK: Ashgate Press, 2004.

Doyle, C. Andrew *A Generous Community: Being the Church in a New Missionary Age.* New York: Morehouse Publishing, 2015.

Figley, Charles R., and William P. Nash, eds. *Combat Stress Injury: Theory, Research, and Management.* New York: Routledge Press, 2007.

Grossman, Dave. *On Killing: The Psychological Cost of Learning to Kill in War and Society.* Boston: Back Bay Books, 1995.

Higgins, Hardie M. *To Make the Wounded Whole: Healing the Spiritual Wounds of PTSD.* West Conshohocken, PA: Infinity Publishing, 2010.

Hill, Peter C., and Ralph W. Hood, Jr. *Measures of Religiosity.* Birmingham, AL: Religious Education Press, 1999.

Hillman, James. *A Terrible Love of War.* New York: Penguin Books, 2004.

James, William. *The Varieties of Religious Experience: A Study in Human Nature.* New York: Penguin Books, 1982.

Jones, Alan. *A Passion for Pilgrimage.* New York: Morehouse, 2000.

Kinghorn, Warren. "Combat Trauma and Moral Fragmentation: A Theological Account of Moral Injury." *Journal of the Society of Christian Ethics* 32 (2012): 57–74.

Levine, Adele. *Run, Don't Walk: The Curious and Chaotic Life of a Physical Therapist at Walter Read Army Medical Center.* New York: Penguin Press, 2014.

MacCulloch, Diarmaid. *Thomas Cranmer: A Life.* New Haven, CT: Yale University Press, 1996.

Maguen, Sheila, and Brett Litz. "Moral Injury in Veterans of War." *PTSD Research Quarterly* 23, no. 1 (2012): 1–6.

Marlantes, Karl. *What It Is Like to Go to War.* New York: Grove Press, 2012.

Meagher, Robert Emmet. *Killing From the Inside Out: Moral Injury and Just War.* Eugene, OR: Cascade Books, 2014.

McNeill, John T., and Helena M. Gamer. *Medieval Handbooks of Penance.* New York: Columbia University Press, 1938.

Moffett-Moore, David. *Life as Pilgrimage: A View from Celtic Spirituality.* South Bend, IN: Cloverdale Books, 2007.

Mullaney, Craig M. *The Unforgiving Minute: A Soldier's Education.* New York: Penguin Books, 2010.

O'Brien, Tim. *The Things They Carried.* Boston: Mariner Books, 2009.

Pauck, Wilhelm and Marion. *Paul Tillich: His Life and Thought.* New York: Harper and Row Publishers, 1976.

Peters, David W. *Death Letter: God, Sex, and War.* Colorado Springs: Tactical16, 2014.

Peterson, Kenneth V. *Prayer as Night Falls: Experiencing Compline.* Brewster, MA: Paraclete Press, 2013.

Ramshaw, Elaine. *Ritual and Pastoral Care.* Philadelphia: Fortress Press, 1989.

Reed, Paul. *Kontum Diary: Captured Writings Bring Peace to a Vietnam Veteran.* Arlington, TX: Summit Publishing Group, 1997.

Robinson, Martin. *Sacred Places, Pilgrim Paths: An Anthology of Pilgrimage.* New York: HarperCollins, 1997.

Shapiro, Francine. *EMDR: The Breakthrough Therapy for Overcoming Anxiety, Stress, and Trauma.* New York: Basic Books, 1997.

Shay, Jonathan. *Achilles in Vietnam: Combat Trauma and the Undoing of Character.* New York: Simon and Schuster, 1995.

————. *Odysseus in America: Combat Trauma and the Trials of Homecoming.* New York: Scribner and Sons, 2003.

Sherrill, Henry Knox. *Among Friends: An Autobiography.* New York: Little and Brown, 1962.

Slone, Laurie B., and Matthew J. Friedman. *After the War Zone: A Practical Guide for Returning Troops and Their Families.* Philadelphia: Da Capo Press, 2008.

Tick, Edward. *War and the Soul: Healing Our Nation's Veterans from Post-Traumatic Stress Disorder.* New York: Quest Books, 2005.

————. *The Practice of Dream Healing: Bringing Ancient Greek Mysteries into Modern Medicine.* Wheaton, IL: Quest Books, 2001.

Tillich, Paul. *Systematic Theology.* Vols. 1–3. Chicago: University of Chicago Press, 1951–63.

Verkamp, Bernard. *The Moral Treatment of Returning Warriors in Early Medieval and Modern Times.* Scranton, PA: University of Scranton Press, 1993.

White, Michael. *C.S. Lewis: A Life.* New York: Carol and Graf Publishers, 2004.

Whitehead, Alfred North. *Process and Reality.* Corrected edition. New York: The Free Press, 1978.